Making Words Second Grade

100 Hands-On Lessons for Phonemic Awareness, Phonics, and Spelling

Patricia M. Cunningham

Wake Forest University

Dorothy P. Hall

Wake Forest University

PEARSON

Boston • New York • San Francisco
Mexico City • Montreal • Toronto • London • Madrid • Munich • Paris
Hong Kong • Singapore • Tokyo • Cape Town • Sydney

Executive Editor: Aurora Martínez Ramos
Series Editorial Assistant: Kara Kikel
Director of Professional Development: Alison Maloney
Marketing Manager: Danae April
Production Editor: Annette Joseph
Editorial Production Service: Lynda Griffiths
Composition Buyer: Linda Cox
Manufacturing Buyer: Linda Morris
Electronic Composition: Denise Hoffman
Interior Design: Denise Hoffman
Cover Administrator: Kristina Mose-Libon

For related titles and support materials, visit our online catalog at www.ablongman.com.

Between the time website information is gathered and then published, it is not unusual for some sites to have closed. Also, the transcription of URLs can result in typographical errors. The publisher would appreciate notification where these errors occur so that they may be corrected in subsequent editions.

ISBN-10: 0-205-58094-7
ISBN-13: 978-0-205-58094-1

Printed in the United States of America

22 2021

Photos: Dorothy P. Hall.

Pat   *Dottie*

Patricia M. Cunningham

From the day I entered first grade, I knew I wanted to be a first-grade teacher. In 1965, I graduated from the University of Rhode Island and began my teaching career teaching first grade in Key West, Florida. For the next several years, I taught a variety of grades and worked as a curriculum coordinator and special reading teacher in Florida and Indiana. From the very beginning, I worried about the children who struggled in learning to read and so I devised a variety of alternative strategies to teach them to read. In 1974, I received my Ph.D. in Reading Education from the University of Georgia.

I developed the Making Words activity while working with Title I teachers in North Carolina, where I was the Director of Reading for Alamance County Schools. I have been the Director of Elementary Education at Wake Forest University in Winston-Salem, North Carolina, since 1980 and have worked with numerous teachers to develop hands-on, engaging ways to teach phonics and spelling. In 1991, I wrote *Phonics They Use: Words for Reading and Writing*, which is currently available in its fourth edition. Along with Richard Allington, I also wrote *Classrooms that Work* and *Schools that Work*.

Dottie Hall and I have worked together on many projects. In 1989, we began developing the Four Blocks Framework, a comprehensive approach to literacy that is used in many schools in the United States and Canada. Dottie and I have produced many books together, including the first *Making Words* books and the *Month by Month Phonics* books. These *Making Words* for grade levels kindergarten to fifth grade are in response to requests by teachers across the years to have Making Words lessons with a scope and sequence tailored to their various grade levels. We hope you and your students will enjoy these Making Words lessons and we would love to hear your comments and suggestions.

Dorothy P. Hall

I always wanted to teach young children. After graduating from Worcester State College in Massachusetts, I taught first and second grades. Two years later, I moved to North Carolina, where I continued teaching in the primary grades. Many children I worked with in the newly integrated schools struggled in learning to read. Wanting to increase my knowledge, I received my M.Ed. and Ed.D. in Reading from the University of North Carolina at Greensboro. I also worked at Wake Forest University, where I met and began to work with Pat Cunningham.

After three years of teaching at the college level I returned to the public schools and taught third and fourth grades and served as a reading and curriculum coordinator for my school district. At this time Pat Cunningham and I began to collaborate on a number of projects. In 1989, we developed the Four Blocks Framework, a comprehensive approach to literacy in grades 1, 2, and 3, which we called Big Blocks. Later, we expanded the program to include kindergarten, calling it Building Blocks. By 1999, Pat and I had written four *Making Words* books, a series of *Month by Month Phonics* books, and *The Teacher's Guide to Four Blocks*, and I retired from the school system to devote more time to consulting and writing. I also went back to work at Wake Forest University, where I taught courses in reading, children's literature, and language arts instruction for elementary education students.

Today, I am Director of the Four Blocks Center at Wake Forest University and enjoy working with teachers and administrators around the country presenting workshops on Four Blocks, Building Blocks, guided reading strategies, and phonics instruction. I have also written several books with teachers. One request Pat and I have had for a number of years is to revise the *Making Words* by grade level and include a scope and sequence for the phonics instruction taught. Here it is—Enjoy!

Contents

Introduction

Many teachers first discovered Making Words in the first edition of *Phonics They Use*, which was published in 1991. Since then, teachers around the world have used Making Words lessons to help children discover how our spelling system works. Making Words lessons are an example of a type of instruction called guided discovery. In order to truly learn and retain strategies, children must discover them. But many children do not make discoveries about words on their own. In Making Words lessons, children are guided to make those discoveries.

Making Words is a popular activity with both teachers and children. Children love manipulating letters to make words and figuring out the secret word that can be made with all the letters. While children are having fun making words, they are also learning important information about phonics and spelling. As children manipulate the letters to make the words, they learn how small changes, such as changing just one letter or moving the letters around, result in completely new words. Children develop phonemic awareness as they stretch out words and listen for the sounds they hear and the order of those sounds.

Teaching a Making Words Lesson

Every Making Words lesson has three parts. First, children manipulate the letters to *make* words. This part of the lesson uses a spelling approach to help children learn letter sounds and how to segment words and blend letters. In the second part of the lesson, children *sort* words according to rhyming patterns. We end each lesson by helping children *transfer* what they have learned to reading and spelling new words. Children learn how the rhyming words they sorted help them read and spell lots of other rhyming words.

Each Making Words lesson begins with short easy words and moves to longer, more complex words. The last word is always the secret word—a word that can be made with all the letters. As children arrange the letters, a child who has successfully made a word goes to the pocket chart and makes the word with big letters. Children who don't have the word made correctly quickly fix their word so that they're ready for the next word. The small changes between most words encourage even those children who have not made a word perfectly to fix it because they soon realize that having the current word correctly spelled increases their chances of spelling the next word correctly. In second grade, each lesson includes 12 to 15 words, including the secret word that can be made with all the letters.

In Part Two of a Making Words lesson, children sort the words into patterns. Many children discover patterns just through making the words in the carefully sequenced order, but some children need more explicit guidance. This guidance happens when all the words have been made and the teacher guides the children to sort them into patterns. Children sort the words into rhyming words and notice that words that rhyme have the same spelling pattern.

Many children know letter sounds and patterns but do not apply these to decode an unknown word encountered during reading or to spell a word they need while writing. This is the reason that every Making Words lesson ends with a transfer step. After words are sorted according to beginning letters, children apply these beginning letter sounds to new words. When words are sorted according to rhyme, children use these rhyming words to decode and spell new words. Here is an example of how you might conduct a Making Words lesson and cue the children to the changes and words you want them to make. (This lesson is #58 in *Making Words Second Grade*.)

Beginning the Lesson

The children all have the letters: **a e u c c k p s**

These same letters—big enough for all to see—are displayed in a pocket chart. The letter cards have lowercase letters on one side and capital letters on the other side. The vowels are in a different color.

The words the children are going to make are written on index cards. These words will be placed in the pocket chart as the words are made and will be used for the Sort and Transfer steps of the lesson.

The teacher begins the lesson by having the children hold up and name each letter as the teacher holds up the big letters in the pocket chart.

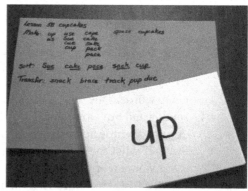

"Hold up and name each letter as I hold up the big letter. Let's start with your vowels. Show me your **a,** your **u,** and your **e.** Now show me your two **c**'s, **k, p,** and **s.** Today you have 8 letters. In a few minutes, we will see if anyone can figure out the secret word that uses all 8 letters."

Part One: Making Words

"Use 2 letters to spell the word **up.** I got **up** at 6:30."

(Find someone with **up** spelled correctly and send that child to spell **up** with the big letters.)

"Change 1 letter to spell **us**. The fifth-graders put on a play for **us**."

"Add a letter you don't hear to spell **use**. We **use** our letters to make words."

"Move the same letters to spell the name **Sue**. Do you know anyone named **Sue**?"

(Find someone with **Sue** spelled with a capital **S** to spell **Sue** with the big letters.)

"Change 1 letter to spell **cue**. When you are an actor, you listen for your **cue**."

(Quickly send someone with the correct spelling to make the word with the big letters. Keep the pace brisk. Do not wait until everyone has **cue** spelled with their little letters. It is fine if some children are making **cue** as **cue** is being spelled with the big letters. Choose your struggling readers to go to the pocket chart when easy words are being spelled and your advanced readers when harder words are being made.)

"Change 1 letter in **cue** to spell **cup**. The baby drinks from a sippy **cup**."

"Change the vowel to spell **cap**. Do you ever wear a **cap**?"

"Add a silent letter to change **cap** into **cape**. Batman wore a **cape**."

"Change 1 letter to spell **cake**. Do you like chocolate **cake**?"

"Change 1 letter to spell **sake**. I hope for your **sake** that it doesn't rain during the game."

"Change the last 2 letters to spell **sack**. A **sack** is another name for a bag."

"Change 1 letter to spell **pack**. **Pack** your clothes for the sleepover."

"Change the last letter to spell another 4 letter word, **pace**. The racers ran at a very fast **pace**."

"Add 1 letter to spell **space**. When we write, we leave a **space** between words."

"I have just one word left. It is the secret word you can make with all your letters. See if you can figure it out."

(Give the children one minute to figure out the secret word. Then give clues if needed.) Let someone who figures it out go to the big letters and spell the secret word: **cupcakes**.

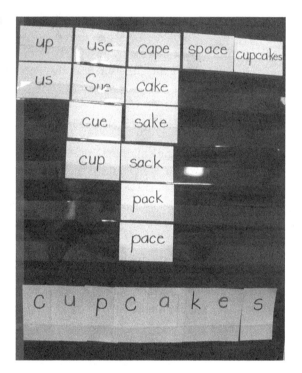

Part Two: Sorting the Words into Patterns

Using the index cards with words you made, place them in the pocket chart as the children pronounce and chorally spell each. Give them a quick reminder of how they made these words:

"First we spelled a 2 letter word, **up**, u-p."

"We changed the last letter to spell **us**, u-s."

"We added the silent e to spell **use**, u-s-e."

"We used the same letters with a capital S to spell **Sue**, S-u-e."

"We changed the first letter to spell **cue**, c-u-e."

"We changed the last letter to spell **cup**, c-u-p."

"We changed the vowel to spell **cap**, c-a-p."

"We added the silent e to spell **cape**, c-a-p-e."

"We changed 1 letter to spell **cake**, c-a-k-e."

"We changed 1 letter to spell **sake**, s-a-k-e."

"We changed 2 letters to spell **sack**, s-a-c-k."

"We changed 1 letter to spell **pack**, p-a-c-k."

"We changed the last letter to spell **pace**, p-a-c-e."

"We added a letter to spell **space**, s-p-a-c-e."

"Finally, we spelled the secret word using all our letters, **cupcakes**, c-u-p-c-a-k-e-s."

Next have the children sort the rhyming words. Take one of each set of rhyming words and place them in the pocket chart.

Sue	cake	pace	sack	cup

Ask three children to find the other words that rhyme and place them under the ones you pulled out.

Sue	cake	pace	sack	cup
cue	sake	space	pack	up

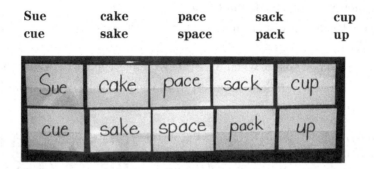

Have the children chorally pronounce the sets of rhyming words.

Part Three: Transfer

Tell the children to pretend it is writing time and they need to spell some words that rhyme with some of the words they made today. Have the children use whiteboards or half-sheets of paper to write the words. Say sentences that children might want to write that include a rhyming word. Work together to decide which words the target word rhymes with and to decide how to spell it.

> "Boys and girls, let's pretend it is writing time. Terry is writing about what he likes to eat for a **snack** and he is trying to spell the word **snack**. Let's all say **snack** and stretch out the beginning letters. What 2 letters do you hear at the beginning of **snack**?"

Have the children stretch out **snack** and listen for the beginning letters. When they tell you that **snack** begins with **sn**, write **sn** on an index card and have the children write **sn** on their papers or whiteboards.

Take the index card with **sn** on it to the pocket chart and hold it under each column of words as you lead the children to chorally pronounce the words and decide if **snack** rhymes with them:

> "Sue, cue, snack." Children should show you "thumbs down."
>
> "Cake, sake, snack." Children should again show you "thumbs down."
>
> "Pace, space, snack." Children should again show you "thumbs down."
>
> "Sack, pack, snack." Children should show you "thumbs up."

Finish writing **snack** on your index card by adding **ack** to **sn** and place **snack** in the pocket chart under **sack** and **pack**.

Make up sentences and use the same procedure to demonstrate how you use **pace** and **space** to spell **brace** and **sack** and **pack** to spell **track**.

We hope this sample lesson has helped you see how a Making Words lesson works and how Making Words lessons help children develop phonemic awareness, phonics, and spelling skills. Most important, we hope you see that in every lesson children will practice applying the patterns they are learning to reading and spelling new words.

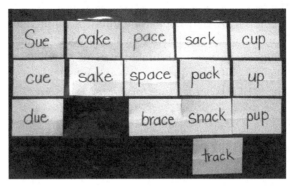
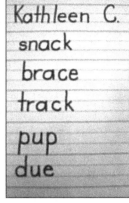

Scope and Sequence for Making Words Second Grade Lessons

Making Words Second Grade contains 100 lessons that teach all the phonics, spelling, and phonemic awareness skills included in most second-grade curriculums. The lessons lead children through a systematic and sequential phonics curriculum. All lessons include practice with the phonemic awareness skills of segmenting and blending as children stretch out words they are making and blend the letters to make new words. Because teaching children letter-sound relationships is easier than teaching children to actually use these letter-sound relationships, all lessons include a transfer step in which children apply the sounds they are learning to spelling new words.

The first 10 lessons teach the common sounds for the vowels and most useful consonants. Lessons 11 to 20 review the vowel sounds and teach the sounds for **sh**, **ch**, **th**, and **ck**. The following lessons systematically teach all the important vowel combinations. After the letter sounds are taught, they continue to be practiced and reviewed in the lessons that follow. You can do the lessons in order or choose lessons that focus on particular letter combinations your students need to learn.

Lessons	Letters/Sounds Taught
Lessons 1–10	*a e i o u er*
Lessons 11–20	*sh ch th ck*
Lessons 21–30	*i-e ie ir igh*
Lessons 31–40	*ai a-e ar ay y*
Lessons 41–50	*ea ee er*
Lessons 51–60	*u ue u-e ur*
Lessons 61–70	*oa o-e or*
Lessons 71–80	*oo oy oi ou*
Lessons 81–90	*ow aw* *all ell ill*
Lessons 91–100	Review

Assessment

After every 10 lessons, there is an assessment that you can use to determine how individual children are growing in their phonics, phonemic awareness, and spelling skills. Record sheets are included to help you monitor each child's progress. In addition to assessing for the new skills taught, you may want to recheck children on items they were not successful at in previous assessments. Reproducible record sheets are included in the back of this book.

Organizing to Teach Making Words

The materials you need to teach a Making Words lesson are quite simple. You need a pocket chart in which to display the word correctly made with the pocket-chart letters. You need a set of pocket-chart letters big enough for all the children to see. Also, you need index cards on which to write the words children will make and the transfer words. Most teachers store their index cards for each lesson in an envelope.

The children need small letter cards and a holder in which to make the words. The letter holder is easily made from half a file folder. The holder is very important to the success of your lesson because it focuses all the children on making their own words. Without the holders, children who are not very fast at making words will simply look at the letters of a quick child seated near them and put down the same letters. The learning in a Making Words lesson does not occur when the child moves the letters. Rather, the

How to Make a Letter Holder

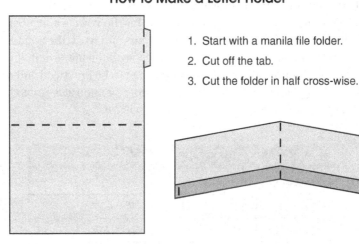

1. Start with a manila file folder.
2. Cut off the tab.
3. Cut the folder in half cross-wise.

Prepare each half of the folder as follows:

4. Fold up one inch on the bottom edge to form a shallow pocket.
5. Press firmly along folded edge with a ruler to flatten.
6. Staple side edges.

You now have a letter holder that your students can set on their desks to put letters in when making words.

learning happens when the child says the word and thinks about where to move the letters. Making Words is a guided discovery activity and you want all your children to engage in the discovery. As the children are making words, walk behind them and select a child with the word made correctly to make the words with the pocket chart letters. Choose your struggling readers to go to the pocket chart and make some of the easier words and they will stay engaged with the lesson because they are experiencing some success. Be sure to ask all children to fix their word if it was not correct when the word is made in the pocket chart.

Another advantage of using the holder is that it allows you to get all the letters quickly out of the hands of the children before the sorting step of the lesson. Have all the children make the secret word in their holder once it is made in the pocket chart. Let them hold up their holders to show you the secret word and then have them close their holders with all the letters in them. They will pay better attention to the sorting activity if they do not still have the letters in front of them to distract them.

A final reason to use the holders is that they are the most efficient way to distribute the letters the children need. When you are going to do a Making Words lesson, put the holders and letters on a table and have the children walk by and pick up a holder and one letter from each plate. We call this "stuffing your holder." When the lesson ends, collect everyone's holder with the letters still in there. At the end of the day, appoint some "holder unstuffer helpers" to take the letters out of the holders and place them on the appropriate plate. Place the letters from each plate into the appropriate zippered bag and you have put everything away— neat and tidy and ready for the next lesson.

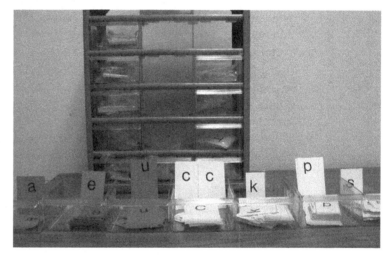

At the back of this book, you will find reproducible letters. Copy these on card stock and cut them with your paper cutter. Use a different color paper for the vowels and a third color for y, which is sometimes a vowel and sometimes a consonant. Make twice as many letters as you have children because some words need two of the same letter.

Making Words Homework

Because children like manipulating the letters and coming up with more words than we have time to make in the lesson, a Making Words Take-Home Sheet is a popular activity. You will find a duplicatable template in the back of this book. Write the letters in the boxes at the top in alphabetical order with vowels and then consonants. Before leaving the classroom, have the children turn the sheet over and write the capital letters on the back. When they get home, the children cut or tear the letters from the top and then fill the boxes with words. They can use words made in class or other words. Children enjoy this homework assignment because they know the secret word and they love watching parents and others try to figure it out!

Making Words Lessons Are Multilevel

Making Words lessons are designed so that all your students, regardless of level, will feel challenged and will experience success. In the example lesson described here, the focus was on the **u**, **u-e**, and **ue** patterns. The lesson, however, included some words that reviewed the sound of **a-e** and **ack** taught much earlier. The inclusion of a secret word—a word that can be made with all the letters—provides a challenge for your most able spellers. From the time they get the letters, they are manipulating them in their minds to try to figure out what word can be spelled with all the letters. Most of your children will not figure out that **a**, **e**, **u**, **c**, **c**, **k**, **p**, and **s** can be put together to spell **cupcakes**, but including a secret word in every lesson makes the lesson multilevel for even your quickest word wizards!

Another way in which Making Words lessons are multilevel involves the three parts of the lesson. We ask children to say each word before they make it and encourage them to stretch out words. This saying and stretching provides crucial practice for children who still need to work on the phonemic awareness skill of segmenting. In the sort segment of the lesson, before we sort the words, we place them in the pocket chart and have the children read the words. As they read the words, children practice the phonemic awareness skill of blending. Sorting the words into beginning letter patterns and rhyming patterns helps children learn the sounds for beginning letters and vowel patterns. Finally, we include a transfer step in every lesson. Children stretch out the transfer word to determine the beginning letters and then use the rhyming words made to spell new words. Every Making Words lesson provides multiple opportunities for children to develop phonemic awareness, learn phonics patterns, and transfer their knowledge to spelling new words. For many years, teachers have enjoyed doing Making Words lessons with their entire class of students, confident in the knowledge that all children, regardless of level, will grow in their phonics, phonemic awareness, and spelling skills as they participate in these active hands-on learning lessons. We hope you and your second-graders enjoy these lessons created just for you and them! (For other phonics lessons tailor-made for second-graders, see *Month by Month Phonics for Second Grade*, by Dorothy P. Hall and Patricia M. Cunningham, published by Carson-Dellosa in 2003.)

Lessons 1-10

These 10 lessons review the most common vowel sounds for **a**, **e**, **i**, **o**, and **u** and **er**.

Lesson 1

planets

Letters: a e l n p s t (Review vowel sounds **a** and **e**.)

Words to Make: at pat pet net ten tan ant sent nest pest
past pant plant planets

Part One • Making Words

Have the children arrange their letters in front of their holders to match the pocket-chart letters, with the vowel first and the other letters in alphabetical order. Have them notice that the vowels are a different color and tell them they will make many new words today by just changing the vowel. Have children hold up and name each letter, noting the capital letter is used to spell names.

at "The first word we are going to spell is **at**. We are **at** school. Everyone say **at**. Use 2 letters to spell **at**."

Choose a child who has **at** spelled correctly to spell **at** with the pocket-chart letters. Have the class chorally spell **at** and fix their word if **at** is not correct.

Pat "Add 1 letter to spell the name **Pat**. My cousin's name is **Pat**. Everyone say **Pat**."

Let a child who has **Pat** spelled with a capital **P** spell **Pat** with the pocket-chart letters.

pet "Change the vowel to spell **pet**. Do you have a **pet**? Everyone say **pet**."

Continue the lesson, giving children explicit instruction about which letters to re-move and where to add letters. Put each word in a sentence and have children say each word before making it. Have them "stretch" some words to provide practice for children who are still learning to segment words. Let a child who has spelled the word correctly make that word with the pocket-chart letters. Choose your struggling readers when the word is an easy word and choose your advanced readers for harder words. Have the children chorally spell each word after it is made in the pocket chart and fix their word to match.

net	"Change the first letter to spell **net**. In tennis, you have to hit the ball over the **net**. Everyone say **net**."
ten	"Use the same letters to spell **ten**. I have **ten** fingers. Everyone say **ten**."
tan	"Change the vowel to spell **tan**. I get a **tan** in the summer. Everyone say **tan**."
ant	"Use the same letters to spell **ant**. I watched the **ant** crawl across the sand. Everyone say **ant**."
sent	"Clear your holders and use 4 letters to spell **sent**. I **sent** a birthday present to my grandma. Everyone say **sent**."
nest	"Use the same letters to spell **nest**. The birds built a **nest**. Everyone say **nest**."
pest	"Change just the first letter to spell **pest**. Don't be a **pest**! Everyone say **pest**."
past	"Change the vowel to spell **past**. I walk **past** the drugstore on my way to school. Everyone say **past**."
pant	"Change just 1 letter to spell **pant**. Does your dog **pant** when it is hot? Everyone say **pant**."
plant	"Add 1 letter to spell **plant**. We **plant** flowers in our garden. Everyone say **plant**."
planets	**(the secret word)** "It's time for the secret word. Move your letters in your holder to figure out the word that can be made with all the letters. Signal me if you think you have it."

If no one makes the secret words in one minute, give them a clue. End the making words part of the lesson by having someone spell **planets** in the pocket chart and letting everyone hold up their holders to show you **planets** made in their holders. Have them close the holders and turn their attention to the pocket chart.

Part Two • Sorting Words (Sort for at, ant, est, and et)

Tell your students that they are going to say all the words they spelled and then sort the rhyming words. Using the index cards with the words, place them in the pocket chart and have the children pronounce them. Remind the children of what they changed to make each word.

"First we used 2 letters to spell **at**, a-t."

"We added a capital **P** to spell the name **Pat**, P-a-t."

"We changed the vowel to spell **pet**, p-e-t."

"We changed the first letter to spell **net**, n-e-t."

"We used the same letters to spell **ten**, t-e-n."

"We changed the vowel to spell **tan**, t-a-n."

"We used the same letters to spell **ant, a-n-t**."

"Next, we spelled a 4 letter word, **sent, s-e-n-t**."

"We used the same letters to spell **nest, n-e-s-t**."

"We changed the first letter to spell **pest, p-e-s-t**."

"We changed the vowel to spell **past, p-a-s-t**."

"We changed the **s** to an **n** to spell **pant, p-a-n-t**."

"We added a letter to spell **plant, p-l-a-n-t**."

"We used all our letters to spell the secret word, **planets, p-l-a-n-e-t-s**."

"Now we need to sort out the rhymes. I will take one of each set and you can come and help me find the others."

Arrange one of each set of rhyming words to begin four columns.

Pat	pant	nest	pet

Choose four children and help them choose the rhyming words and line them up in columns. Have the rhyming words pronounced and have children notice that they all rhyme and they all have the same letters from the vowel to the end of the word.

Pat	pant	nest	pet
at	plant	pest	net
	ant		

Part Three • Transfer west grant flat vet

Have the children take out paper. Tell them that you are going to say a word that someone might be writing. By figuring out the rhyming pattern, they will be able to spell the word.

"The first word we are going to spell is **west**. David might be writing about a trip out **west**. Let's all say **west** and listen for the beginning letters."

Write **w** on an index card when the children decide that **west** begins with **w**. Take the index card to the pocket chart and have the children pronounce **west** with each set of rhyming words. When they decide that **west** rhymes with **pest** and **nest**, write **est** next to **w**. Have the children write **west** on their papers.

Repeat this procedure for **grant, flat,** and **vet**.

Lesson 2

absent

Letters: | a | e | b | n | s | t | (Review vowel sounds **a** and **e**.)

Make: at bat sat set net ten tan ban Ben bent best
nest sent absent

Sort:
at	net	Ben	nest	tan	sent
bat	set	ten	best	ban	bent
sat					absent

Transfer: spent   vest   plan   scat

Make Words

- Have children name and hold up letters.
- Tell children how many letters to use to make each word.
- Have children say each word and stretch out some words.
- Give sentences to clarify meaning.
- Give specific instructions on how to change words:
  — Add one letter.
  — Change the first letter.
  — Use the same letters.
- Have children clear their holders before making an unrelated word.
- Be sure children use capital letters when spelling **Ben**.
- Have children correct their word once it is made in the pocket chart.
- Give children one minute to figure out the secret word and then give them clues.

Sort Words

- Put words in pocket chart in the order made.
- Have children say and spell each word.
- Remind them of how each word was changed to spell the new word.
- Select one word from each rhyming set and line up in columns.
- Let children come and choose the other words that rhyme.
- Have children pronounce the words.

Transfer Words

- Tell the children that they are going to use the rhyming words to spell some new words they might need when they are writing.
- Say the word and a sentence one of your children might write.
- Have children say the word and decide on the beginning letters.
- Write the beginning letters on an index card.
- Take the index card with the beginning letters to the pocket chart and have children say the columns of rhymes and the new word to find the rhyming pattern.
- Write the rhyming pattern on the card to finish the word.
- Have students write the word on paper or a whiteboard.

Lesson 3

blankets

Letters: | a | e | b | l | k | n | s | t | (Review vowel sounds **a** and **e**)

Make: sat bat bet net nest best last tank sank bank
blank blast absent basket blankets

Sort:

bank	bet	best	last	sat
sank	net	nest	blast	bat
blank	basket			
tank				

Transfer: fast prank plank vest

Make Words

- Have children name and hold up letters.
- Tell children how many letters to use to make each word.
- Have children say each word and stretch out some words.
- Give sentences to clarify meaning.
- Give specific instructions on how to change words:
  — Add one letter.
  — Change the first letter.
  — Use the same letters.
- Have children clear their holders before making an unrelated word.
- Have children correct their word once it is made in the pocket chart.
- Give children one minute to figure out the secret word and then give them clues.

Sort Words

- Put words in pocket chart in the order made.
- Have children say and spell each word.
- Remind them of how each word was changed to spell the new word.
- Select one word from each rhyming set and line up in columns.
- Let children choose the other words that rhyme.
- Have children pronounce the words.

Transfer Words

- Tell children that they are going to use the rhyming words to spell some new words they might need when they are writing.
- Say the word and a sentence one of your children might write.
- Have children say the word and decide on the beginning letters.
- Write the beginning letters on an index card.
- Take the index card with the beginning letters to the pocket chart and have children say the columns of rhymes and the new word to find the rhyming pattern.
- Write the rhyming pattern on the card to finish the word.
- Have students write the word on paper or a whiteboard.

Lesson 4

napkins

Letters: | a | i | k | n | n | p | s | (Review vowel sounds **a** and **i**.)

Make: in an pan pin nip nap snap snip spin skin sink
pink sank spank napkins

Sort:

an	nip	in	pink	spank	snap
pan	snip	pin	sink	sank	nap
		spin			
		skin			

Transfer: blink yank stink flap

Make Words

- Have children name and hold up letters.
- Tell children how many letters to use to make each word.
- Have children say each word and stretch out some words.
- Give sentences to clarify meaning.
- Give specific instructions on how to change words:
  — Add one letter.
  — Change the first letter.
  — Use the same letters.
- Have children clear their holders before making an unrelated word.
- Have children correct their word once it is made in the pocket chart.
- Give children one minute to figure out the secret word and then give them clues.

Sort Words

- Put words in pocket chart in the order made.
- Have children say and spell each word.
- Remind them of how each word was changed to spell the new word.
- Select one word from each rhyming set and line up in columns.
- Let children choose the other words that rhyme.
- Have children pronounce the words.

Transfer Words

- Tell children that they are going to use the rhyming words to spell some new words they might need when they are writing.
- Say the word and a sentence one of your children might write.
- Have children say the word and decide on the beginning letters.
- Write the beginning letters on an index card.
- Take the index card with the beginning letters to the pocket chart and have children say the columns of rhymes and the new word to find the rhyming pattern.
- Write the rhyming pattern on the card to finish the word.
- Have students write the word on paper or a whiteboard.

Lesson 5

husband

Letters: | a | u | b | d | h | n | s | (Review vowel sounds **a** and **u**.)

Make: us bus sub sun bun ban bad bud had and hand sand band husband

Sort:

bad	bus	sand	bun
had	us	band	sun
		hand	
		and	
		husband	

Transfer: grand glad brand run

Make Words

- Have children name and hold up letters.
- Tell children how many letters to use to make each word.
- Have children say each word and stretch out some words.
- Give sentences to clarify meaning.
- Give specific instructions on how to change words:
  — Add one letter.
  — Change the first letter.
  — Use the same letters.
- Have children clear their holders before making an unrelated word.
- Have children correct their word once it is made in the pocket chart.
- Give children one minute to figure out the secret word and then give them clues.

Sort Words

- Put words in pocket chart in the order made.
- Have children say and spell each word.
- Remind them of how each word was changed to spell the new word.
- Select one word from each rhyming set and line up in columns.
- Let children choose the other words that rhyme.
- Have children pronounce the words.

Transfer Words

- Tell children that they are going to use the rhyming words to spell some new words they might need when they are writing.
- Say the word and a sentence one of your children might write.
- Have children say the word and decide on the beginning letters.
- Write the beginning letters on an index card.
- Take the index card with the beginning letters to the pocket chart and have children say the columns of rhymes and the new word to find the rhyming pattern.
- Write the rhyming pattern on the card to finish the word.
- Have students write the word on paper or a whiteboard.

Lesson 6

trusting

Letters: | i | u | g | n | r | s | t | t | (Review vowel sounds **i** and **u**.)

Make: us Gus rig rug tug ring rung rust trust sting
stung strung string rusting trusting

Sort:

ring	tug	us	rung	rust	rusting
sting	rug	Gus	stung	trust	trusting
string			strung		

Transfer: spring must dusting mug

Make Words

- Have children name and hold up letters.
- Tell children how many letters to use to make each word.
- Have children say each word and stretch out some words.
- Give sentences to clarify meaning.
- Give specific instructions on how to change words:
  — Add one letter.
  — Change the first letter.
  — Use the same letters.
- Have children clear their holders before making an unrelated word.
- Be sure children use a capital letter when spelling **Gus**.
- Have children correct their word once it is made in the pocket chart.
- Give children one minute to figure out the secret word and then give them clues.

Sort Words

- Put words in pocket chart in the order made.
- Have children say and spell each word.
- Remind them of how each word was changed to spell the new word.
- Select one word from each rhyming set and line up in columns.
- Let children choose the other words that rhyme.
- Have children pronounce the words.

Transfer Words

- Tell children that they are going to use the rhyming words to spell some new words they might need when they are writing.
- Say the word and a sentence one of your children might write.
- Have children say the word and decide on the beginning letters.
- Write the beginning letters on an index card.
- Take the index card with the beginning letters to the pocket chart and have children say the columns of rhymes and the new word to find the rhyming pattern.
- Write the rhyming pattern on the card to finish the word.
- Have students write the word on paper or a whiteboard.

Lesson 7

contests

 Letters: | e | o | c | n | s | s | t | t | (Review vowel sounds **e** and **o**.)

 Make: on   con   cot   not   net   set   sent   nest   test   tent
              tents   tests   contest   contests

Sort:

nest	con	cot	net	sent
test	on	not	set	tent
contest				

Transfer: trot   west   dent   wet

Make Words

- Have children name and hold up letters.
- Tell children how many letters to use to make each word.
- Have children say each word and stretch out some words.
- Give sentences to clarify meaning.
- Give specific instructions on how to change words:
  — Add one letter.
  — Change the first letter.
  — Use the same letters.
- Have children clear their holders before making an unrelated word.
- Have children correct their word once it is made in the pocket chart.
- Give children one minute to figure out the secret word and then give them clues.

Sort Words

- Put words in pocket chart in the order made.
- Have children say and spell each word.
- Remind them of how each word was changed to spell the new word.
- Select one word from each rhyming set and line up in columns.
- Let children choose the other words that rhyme.
- Have children pronounce the words.

Transfer Words

- Tell children that they are going to use the rhyming words to spell some new words they might need when they are writing.
- Say the word and a sentence one of your children might write.
- Have children say the word and decide on the beginning letters.
- Write the beginning letters on an index card.
- Take the index card with the beginning letters to the pocket chart and have children say the columns of rhymes and the new word to find the rhyming pattern.
- Write the rhyming pattern on the card to finish the word.
- Have students write the word on paper or a whiteboard.

Lesson 8

stopped

Letters: e o d p p s t (Review vowel sounds o and e.)

Make: set pet pot pop pep step stop spot tops pots
pets pest stopped

Sort:
pop	pet	pot	pep
stop	set	spot	step

Transfer: vet drop flop

Make Words

- Have children name and hold up letters.
- Tell children how many letters to use to make each word.
- Have children say each word and stretch out some words.
- Give sentences to clarify meaning.
- Give specific instructions on how to change words:
  — Add one letter.
  — Change the first letter.
  — Use the same letters.
- Have children clear their holders before making an unrelated word.
- Have children correct their word once it is made in the pocket chart.
- Give children one minute to figure out the secret word and then give them clues.

Sort Words

- Put words in pocket chart in the order made.
- Have children say and spell each word.
- Remind them of how each word was changed to spell the new word.
- Select one word from each rhyming set and line up in columns.
- Let children choose the other words that rhyme.
- Have children pronounce the words.

Transfer Words

- Tell children that they are going to use the rhyming words to spell some new words they might need when they are writing.
- Say the word and a sentence one of your children might write.
- Have children say the word and decide on the beginning letters.
- Write the beginning letters on an index card.
- Take the index card with the beginning letters to the pocket chart and have children say the columns of rhymes and the new word to find the rhyming pattern.
- Write the rhyming pattern on the card to finish the word.
- Have students write the word on paper or a whiteboard.

Lesson 9

hunters

Letters: e   u   h   n   r   s   t   (Review vowel sounds **e** and **u** and **er**.)

Make: us   run   sun   nut   net   ten   hen   her   nest   rest
rust   runt   hunt   hunters

Sort:

run	nest	runt	ten
sun	rest	hunt	hen

Transfer: stunt   stun   crest

Make Words

- Have children name and hold up letters.
- Tell children how many letters to use to make each word.
- Have children say each word and stretch out some words.
- Give sentences to clarify meaning.
- Give specific instructions on how to change words:
  — Add one letter.
  — Change the first letter.
  — Use the same letters.
- Have children clear their holders before making an unrelated word.
- Have children correct their word once it is made in the pocket chart.
- Give children one minute to figure out the secret word and then give them clues.

Sort Words

- Put words in pocket chart in the order made.
- Have children say and spell each word.
- Remind them of how each word was changed to spell the new word.
- Select one word from each rhyming set and line up in columns.
- Let children choose the other words that rhyme.
- Have children pronounce the words.

Transfer Words

- Tell children that they are going to use the rhyming words to spell some new words they might need when they are writing.
- Say the word and a sentence one of your children might write.
- Have children say the word and decide on the beginning letters.
- Write the beginning letters on an index card.
- Take the index card with the beginning letters to the pocket chart and have children say the columns of rhymes and the new word to find the rhyming pattern.
- Write the rhyming pattern on the card to finish the word.
- Have students write the word on paper or a whiteboard.

Lesson 10

printers

Letters: [e] [i] [n] [p] [r] [r] [s] [t] (Review vowel sounds **e** and **i**.)

Make: it   in   pin   pit   pet   set   sit   sip   tip   trip   strip
print   stern   insert   printers

Sort:

it	set	sip	in
pit	pet	trip	pin
sit		tip	
		strip	

Transfer: spin   grip   pit   yet

Make Words

- Have children name and hold up letters.
- Tell children how many letters to use to make each word.
- Have children say each word and stretch out some words.
- Give sentences to clarify meaning.
- Give specific instructions on how to change words:
  — Add one letter.
  — Change the first letter.
  — Use the same letters.
- Have children clear their holders before making an unrelated word.
- Have children correct their word once it is made in the pocket chart.
- Give children one minute to figure out the secret word and then give them clues.

Sort Words

- Put words in pocket chart in the order made.
- Have children say and spell each word.
- Remind them of how each word was changed to spell the new word.
- Select one word from each rhyming set and line up in columns.
- Let children choose the other words that rhyme.
- Have children pronounce the words.

Transfer Words

- Tell children that they are going to use the rhyming words to spell some new words they might need when they are writing.
- Say the word and a sentence one of your children might write.
- Have children say the word and decide on the beginning letters.
- Write the beginning letters on an index card.
- Take the index card with the beginning letters to the pocket chart and have children say the columns of rhymes and the new word to find the rhyming pattern.
- Write the rhyming pattern on the card to finish the word.
- Have students write the word on paper or a whiteboard.

Tell the children to pretend they are writing and need to spell some words. To spell the word, they should stretch out the word and write the beginning letters and then decide which rhyming words will help them finish writing the word. Remind them that this is exactly what they do in the transfer step of each Making Words lesson but now you want to see if they can do it on their own.

Write these words in columns and have your students chorally pronounce and spell them. Have them notice that each column of words has the same letters from the vowel to the end of the words and that the words in the column rhyme.

tip	stop	set
rip	pop	pet
trip	top	net

Have the children number a sheet of paper from 1 to 5. Say a word and put it in a sentence. Ask your students to stretch out each word to hear the beginning letters and then decide which words it rhymes with to finish spelling the word:

drip   yet   prop   skip   crop

Record their responses on your record sheet. If students did not use the correct pattern or beginning letters, record what they did use and analyze their errors.

Word	Beginning Letters	Rhyming Pattern
After Lesson 10		
drip	dr	ip
yet	y	et
prop	pr	op
skip	sk	ip
crop	cr	op

Here is one child's record sheet filled in after the assessment.

Kathleen C.

Word	Beginning Letters		Rhyming Pattern	
After Lesson 10				
drip	dr	✓	ip	✓
yet	y	✓	et	✓
prop	pr	✓	op	✓
skip	sk	✓	ip	✓
crop	cr	ch	op	✓

Lessons 11-20

These 10 lessons review the most common vowel sounds and **sh**, **ch**, **ck**, and **th**.

Lesson 11

thinks

Letters: i h k n s t (Sound of **th**)

Words to Make: in it hit sit kit ink sink skin thin hint stink think thinks

Part One • Making Words

 Have the children arrange their letters in front of their holders to match the pocket-chart letters, with the vowel first and the other letters in alphabetical order. Ask the children to hold up and name each letter, noting the capital letter is used to spell names. Ask them to hold up the **t** and the **h** and remind them of the sound these two letters make together.

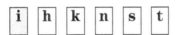

in   "The first word we are going to spell is **in**. We are **in** second grade. Everyone say **in**. Use 2 letters to spell **in**."

Choose a child who has **in** spelled correctly to spell **in** with the pocket-chart letters. Have the class chorally spell **in** and fix their word if **in** is not correct.

it   "Change 1 letter to spell **it**. I lost my key and am looking for **it**. Everyone say **it**."

Let a child who has **it** spelled correctly spell **it** with the pocket-chart letters.

hit   "Add a letter to spell **hit**. He **hit** the ball over the fence. Everyone say **hit**."

Continue the lesson, giving children explicit instruction about which letters to remove and where to add letters. Put each word in a sentence and have children say each word before making it. Have them "stretch" some words to provide practice for children who are still learning to segment words. Let a child who has spelled the word correctly

make that word with the pocket-chart letters. Choose your struggling readers when the word is an easy word and your advanced readers for harder words. Have the children chorally spell each word after it is made in the pocket chart and fix their word to match.

sit	"Change the first letter to spell **sit**. Please **sit** down. Everyone say **sit**."
kit	"Change the first letter to spell **kit**. I built the model airplane from a **kit**. Everyone say **kit**."
ink	"Use 3 letters to spell **ink**. My pen ran out of **ink**. Everyone say **ink**."
sink	"Add 1 letter to spell **sink**. Wash your hands in the **sink**. Everyone say **sink**."
skin	"Use the same 4 letters to spell **skin**. **Skin** covers and protects your body. Everyone say **skin**."
thin	"Change the first 2 letters to spell **thin**. I like **thin** crust pizza. Everyone say **thin**."
hint	"Use the same 4 letters to spell **hint**. Can you give me a **hint** about my birthday present? Everyone say **hint**."
stink	"Clear your holders and use 5 letters to spell **stink**. Does your dog ever **stink** when he is wet? Everyone say **stink**."
think	"Change the first 2 letters to spell **think**. We **think** about how to spell each word. Everyone say **think**."
thinks	**(the secret word)** "It's time for the secret word. I bet everyone can get it today. Add your **s** to **think** and **think** about what the secret word is."

End the making words part of the lesson by having someone spell **thinks** in the pocket chart and letting everyone hold up their holders to show you **thinks** made in their holders. Have them close the holders and turn their attention to the pocket chart.

Part Two • Sorting Words (Sort for the patterns **ink**, **in**, and **sit**.)

Tell your students that they are going to say all the words they spelled and then sort the rhyming words. Using the index cards with the words, place them in the pocket chart and have the children pronounce them. Remind them of what they changed to make each word.

"First we used 2 letters to spell **in**, **i-n**."

"We changed the last letter to spell **it**, **i-t**."

"We added the **h** to spell **hit**, **h-i-t**."

"We changed the first letter to spell **sit**, **s-i-t**."

"We changed the first letter again to spell **kit**, **k-i-t**."

"We used 3 letters to spell **ink**, **i-n-k**."

"We added the **s** to spell **sink**, **s-i-n-k**."

"We used the same letters to spell **skin**, **s-k-i-n**."

"We used four letters including our **th** to spell **thin**, **t-h-i-n**."

"We used the same 4 letters to spell **hint**, **h-i-n-t**."

"We used 5 letters to spell **stink**, **s-t-i-n-k**."

"We changed the first 2 letters to spell **think**, **t-h-i-n-k**."

"We used all our letters to spell the secret word, **thinks**, **t-h-i-n-k-s**."

"Now we need to sort out the rhymes. I will take one of each set and you can come and help me find the others."

Arrange one of each set of rhyming words to begin three columns.

ink	**in**	**sit**

Choose three children and help them choose the rhyming words and line them up in columns. Have the rhyming words pronounced and have children notice that they all rhyme and they all have the same letters from the vowel to the end of the word.

ink	**in**	**sit**
sink	**skin**	**hit**
stink	**thin**	**it**
think		**kit**

Part Three • Transfer   pink   spin   drink   spit

Have the children take out paper. Tell them that you are going to say a word that someone might be writing. By figuring out the rhyming pattern, they will be able to spell the word.

"The first word we are going to spell is **pink**. Kathleen might be writing that her favorite color is **pink**. Let's all say **pink** and listen for the beginning letters."

Write **p** on an index card when the children decide that **pink** begins with **p**. Take the index card to the pocket chart and have the children pronounce **pink** with each set of rhyming words. When they decide that **pink** rhymes with **ink**, **sink**, **think**, and **stink**, write **ink** next to **p**. Have the children write **pink** on their papers.

Repeat this procedure for **spin**, **drip**, and **spit**.

Lesson 12
thanks

Letters: a h k n s t (Sound of th)

Make: at as has hat sat ask ant tan than task
tank sank thank thanks

Sort:

at	ask	tank	as	tan
hat	task	sank	has	than
sat		thank		

Transfer: mask prank brat van

Make Words

- Have children name and hold up letters.
- Tell children how many letters to use to make each word.
- Have children say each word and stretch out some words.
- Give sentences to clarify meaning.
- Give specific instructions on how to change words:
  — Add one letter.
  — Change the first letter.
  — Use the same letters.
- Have children clear their holders before making an unrelated word.
- Have children correct their word once it is made in the pocket chart.
- Give children one minute to figure out the secret word and then give them clues.

Sort Words

- Put words in pocket chart in the order made.
- Have children say and spell each word.
- Remind them of how each word was changed to spell the new word.
- Select one word from each rhyming set and line up in columns.
- Let children choose the other words that rhyme.
- Have children pronounce the words.

Transfer Words

- Tell children that they are going to use the rhyming words to spell some new words they might need when they are writing.
- Say the word and a sentence one of your children might write.
- Have children say the word and decide on the beginning letters.
- Write the beginning letters on an index card.
- Take the index card with the beginning letters to the pocket chart and have children say the columns of rhymes and the new word to find the rhyming pattern.
- Write the rhyming pattern on the card to finish the word.
- Have students write the word on paper or a whiteboard.

Lesson 13
chipmunk

Letters: `i` `u` `c` `h` `k` `m` `n` `p`   (Sound of **ch**)

Make: in up cup pin nip chip chin inch much munch
punch pinch chipmunk

Sort:

in	munch	pinch	nip	cup
pin	punch	inch	chip	up
chin				

Transfer: lunch   thin   crunch   trip

Make Words

- Have children name and hold up letters.
- Tell children how many letters to use to make each word.
- Have children say each word and stretch out some words.
- Give sentences to clarify meaning.
- Give specific instructions on how to change words:
  — Add one letter.
  — Change the first letter.
  — Use the same letters.
- Have children clear their holders before making an unrelated word.
- Have children correct their word once it is made in the pocket chart.
- Give children one minute to figure out the secret word and then give them clues.

Sort Words

- Put words in pocket chart in the order made.
- Have children say and spell each word.
- Remind them of how each word was changed to spell the new word.
- Select one word from each rhyming set and line up in columns.
- Let children choose the other words that rhyme.
- Have children pronounce the words.

Transfer Words

- Tell children that they are going to use the rhyming words to spell some new words they might need when they are writing.
- Say the word and a sentence one of your children might write.
- Have children say the word and decide on the beginning letters.
- Write the beginning letters on an index card.
- Take the index card with the beginning letters to the pocket chart and have children say the columns of rhymes and the new word to find the rhyming pattern.
- Write the rhyming pattern on the card to finish the word.
- Have students write the word on paper or a whiteboard.

Lesson 14

children

Letters: | e | i | c | d | h | l | n | r | (Sound of **ch**)

Make: in Ed red rid hid lid led Ned den end her
herd chin inch children

Sort:

red	hid	in
Ed	lid	chin
led		
Ned		

Transfer: spin   skid   sled   twin

Make Words

- Have children name and hold up letters.
- Tell children how many letters to use to make each word.
- Have children say each word and stretch out some words.
- Give sentences to clarify meaning.
- Give specific instructions on how to change words:
  — Add one letter.
  — Change the first letter.
  — Use the same letters.
- Have children clear their holders before making an unrelated word.
- Make sure children spell **Ed** and **Ned** with capital letters.
- Have children correct their word once it is made in the pocket chart.
- Give children one minute to figure out the secret word and then give them clues.

Sort Words

- Put words in pocket chart in the order made.
- Have children say and spell each word.
- Remind them of how each word was changed to spell the new word.
- Select one word from each rhyming set and line up in columns.
- Let children choose the other words that rhyme.
- Have children pronounce the words.

Transfer Words

- Tell children that they are going to use the rhyming words to spell some new words they might need when they are writing.
- Say the word and a sentence one of your children might write.
- Have children say the word and decide on the beginning letters.
- Write the beginning letters on an index card.
- Take the index card with the beginning letters to the pocket chart and have children say the columns of rhymes and the new word to find the rhyming pattern.
- Write the rhyming pattern on the card to finish the word.
- Have students write the word on paper or a whiteboard.

Lesson 15
brushing

Letters: i u b g h n r s (Sound of **sh**)

Make: us bus sub rub rug rig ring rung sung sing
rush brush shrub shrug brushing

Sort:

us	rub	sung	sing	rush	rug
bus	sub	rung	ring	brush	shrug
	shrub				

Transfer: spring club crush plus

Make Words

- Have children name and hold up letters.
- Tell children how many letters to use to make each word.
- Have children say each word and stretch out some words.
- Give sentences to clarify meaning.
- Give specific instructions on how to change words:
  — Add one letter.
  — Change the first letter.
  — Use the same letters.
- Have children clear their holders before making an unrelated word.
- Have children correct their word once it is made in the pocket chart.
- Give children one minute to figure out the secret word and then give them clues.

Sort Words

- Put words in pocket chart in the order made.
- Have children say and spell each word.
- Remind them of how each word was changed to spell the new word.
- Select one word from each rhyming set and line up in columns.
- Let children choose the other words that rhyme.
- Have children pronounce the words.

Transfer Words

- Tell children that they are going to use the rhyming words to spell some new words they might need when they are writing.
- Say the word and a sentence one of your children might write.
- Have children say the word and decide on the beginning letters.
- Write the beginning letters on an index card.
- Take the index card with the beginning letters to the pocket chart and have children say the columns of rhymes and the new word to find the rhyming pattern.
- Write the rhyming pattern on the card to finish the word.
- Have students write the word on paper or a whiteboard.

Lesson 16

bathtubs

Letters: a u b b h s t t (Sound of **th**)

Make: as us bus sub tub tab bat sat hat hut but shut that bath bathtubs

Sort:

hat	bus	hut	tub
that	us	but	sub
bat		shut	
sat			

Transfer: chat scrub club cut

Make Words

- Have children name and hold up letters.
- Tell children how many letters to use to make each word.
- Have children say each word and stretch out some words.
- Give sentences to clarify meaning.
- Give specific instructions on how to change words:
  — Add one letter.
  — Change the first letter.
  — Use the same letters.
- Have children clear their holders before making an unrelated word.
- Have children correct their word once it is made in the pocket chart.
- Give children one minute to figure out the secret word and then give them clues.

Sort Words

- Put words in pocket chart in the order made.
- Have children say and spell each word.
- Remind them of how each word was changed to spell the new word.
- Select one word from each rhyming set and line up in columns.
- Let children choose the other words that rhyme.
- Have children pronounce the words.

Transfer Words

- Tell children that they are going to use the rhyming words to spell some new words they might need when they are writing.
- Say the word and a sentence one of your children might write.
- Have children say the word and decide on the beginning letters.
- Write the beginning letters on an index card.
- Take the index card with the beginning letters to the pocket chart and have children say the columns of rhymes and the new word to find the rhyming pattern.
- Write the rhyming pattern on the card to finish the word.
- Have students write the word on paper or a whiteboard.

Lesson 17

stockings

Letters: | i | o | c | g | k | n | t | s | s | (Sound of **ck**)

Make: sat cat cot cost cast song sing sink sick sock
Nick tick stick stock stockings

Sort:

sat	sock	stick
cat	stock	sick
		tick
		Nick

Transfer: clock   chick   block   chat

Make Words

- Have children name and hold up letters.
- Tell children how many letters to use to make each word.
- Have children say each word and stretch out some words.
- Give sentences to clarify meaning.
- Give specific instructions on how to change words:
  — Add one letter.
  — Change the first letter.
  — Use the same letters.
- Have children clear their holders before making an unrelated word.
- Make sure children use a capital **N** when spelling **Nick**.
- Have children correct their word once it is made in the pocket chart.
- Give children one minute to figure out the secret word and then give them clues.

Sort Words

- Put words in pocket chart in the order made.
- Have children say and spell each word.
- Remind them of how each word was changed to spell the new word.
- Select one word from each rhyming set and line up in columns.
- Let children choose the other words that rhyme.
- Have children pronounce the words.

Transfer Words

- Tell children that they are going to use the rhyming words to spell some new words they might need when they are writing.
- Say the word and a sentence one of your children might write.
- Have children say the word and decide on the beginning letters.
- Write the beginning letters on an index card.
- Take the index card with the beginning letters to the pocket chart and have children say the columns of rhymes and the new word to find the rhyming pattern.
- Write the rhyming pattern on the card to finish the word.
- Have students write the word on paper or a whiteboard.

Lesson 18

kitchen

Letters: [e] [i] [c] [h] [k] [n] [t]   (Sounds of **ch** and **ck**)

Make: in   tin   ten   Ken   hen   then   thin   chin   inch   neck
Nick   tick   thick   kitchen

Sort:

in	Ken	tick
tin	hen	thick
thin	ten	Nick
chin	then	
	kitchen	

Transfer: brick   click   chick   spin

Make Words

- Have children name and hold up letters.
- Tell children how many letters to use to make each word.
- Have children say each word and stretch out some words.
- Give sentences to clarify meaning.
- Give specific instructions on how to change words:
  — Add one letter.
  — Change the first letter.
  — Use the same letters.
- Have children clear their holders before making an unrelated word.
- Make sure children use capital letters when spelling names.
- Have children correct their word once it is made in the pocket chart.
- Give children one minute to figure out the secret word and then give them clues.

Sort Words

- Put words in pocket chart in the order made.
- Have children say and spell each word.
- Remind them of how each word was changed to spell the new word.
- Select one word from each rhyming set and line up in columns.
- Let children choose the other words that rhyme.
- Have children pronounce the words.

Transfer Words

- Tell children that they are going to use the rhyming words to spell some new words they might need when they are writing.
- Say the word and a sentence one of your children might write.
- Have children say the word and decide on the beginning letters.
- Write the beginning letters on an index card.
- Take the index card with the beginning letters to the pocket chart and have children say the columns of rhymes and the new word to find the rhyming pattern.
- Write the rhyming pattern on the card to finish the word.
- Have students write the word on paper or a whiteboard.

Lesson 19

chickens

Letters: | e | i | c | c | h | k | n | s | (Sounds of **ch** and **ck**)

Make: hen Ken kin ink sink skin chin inch sick Nick
neck check chick inches chickens

Sort:

check	sick	ink	kin	hen
neck	chick	sink	skin	Ken
	Nick		chin	

Transfer: thin   think   thick   speck

Make Words

- Have children name and hold up letters.
- Tell children how many letters to use to make each word.
- Have children say each word and stretch out some words.
- Give sentences to clarify meaning.
- Give specific instructions on how to change words:
  — Add one letter.
  — Change the first letter.
  — Use the same letters.
- Have children clear their holders before making an unrelated word.
- Make sure children use capital letters when spelling names.
- Have children correct their word once it is made in the pocket chart.
- Give children one minute to figure out the secret word and then give them clues.

Sort Words

- Put words in pocket chart in the order made.
- Have children say and spell each word.
- Remind them of how each word was changed to spell the new word.
- Select one word from each rhyming set and line up in columns.
- Let children choose the other words that rhyme.
- Have children pronounce the words.

Transfer Words

- Tell children that they are going to use the rhyming words to spell some new words they might need when they are writing.
- Say the word and a sentence one of your children might write.
- Have children say the word and decide on the beginning letters.
- Write the beginning letters on an index card.
- Take the index card with the beginning letters to the pocket chart and have children say the columns of rhymes and the new word to find the rhyming pattern.
- Write the rhyming pattern on the card to finish the word.
- Have students write the word on paper or a whiteboard.

Lesson 20
chopsticks

Letters: i o c c h k p t s s (Sounds of **ch** and **ck**)

Make: hop shop chop chip ship pick tick sick sock
shock stock stick thick chick chopsticks

Sort:

hop	chip	tick	shock
chop	ship	pick	stock
shop		sick	sock
		stick	
		thick	
		chick	

Transfer: kick trick flock flip

Make Words

- Have children name and hold up letters.
- Tell children how many letters to use to make each word.
- Have children say each word and stretch out some words.
- Give sentences to clarify meaning.
- Give specific instructions on how to change words:
  — Add one letter.
  — Change the first letter.
  — Use the same letters.
- Have children clear their holders before making an unrelated word.
- Have children correct their word once it is made in the pocket chart.
- Give children one minute to figure out the secret word and then give them clues.

Sort Words

- Put words in pocket chart in the order made.
- Have children say and spell each word.
- Remind them of how each word was changed to spell the new word.
- Select one word from each rhyming set and line up in columns.
- Let children choose the other words that rhyme.
- Have children pronounce the words.

Transfer Words

- Tell children that they are going to use the rhyming words to spell some new words they might need when they are writing.
- Say the word and a sentence one of your children might write.
- Have children say the word and decide on the beginning letters.
- Write the beginning letters on an index card.
- Take the index card with the beginning letters to the pocket chart and have children say the columns of rhymes and the new word to find the rhyming pattern.
- Write the rhyming pattern on the card to finish the word.
- Have students write the word on paper or a whiteboard.

Tell the children to pretend they are writing and need to spell some words. To spell the word, they should stretch out the word and write the beginning letters and then decide which rhyming words will help them finish writing the word. Remind them that this is exactly what they do in the transfer step of each Making Words lesson but now you want to see if they can do it on their own.

Write these words in columns and have your students chorally pronounce and spell them. Have them notice that each column of words has the same letters from the vowel to the end of the words and that the words in the column rhyme.

neck	sock	sick
deck	rock	pick
peck	lock	Nick

Have the children number a sheet of paper from 1 to 5. Say a word and put it in a sentence. Ask your students to stretch out each word to hear the beginning letters and then decide which words it rhymes with to finish spelling the word:

thick   check   shock   brick   clock

Record their responses on your record sheet. If students did not use the correct pattern or beginning letters, record what they did use and analyze their errors.

Word	Beginning Letters	Rhyming Pattern
After Lesson 10		
drip	dr	ip
yet	y	et
prop	pr	op
skip	sk	ip
crop	cr	op
After Lesson 20		
thick	th	ick
check	ch	eck
shock	sh	ock
brick	br	ick
clock	cl	ock

Lessons 21-30

These 10 lessons teach the common vowel patterns **ie**, **i-e**, **ir**, and **igh**.

Lesson 21
drivers

Letters: e i d r r s v (Vowel patterns **ide**, **ise**, and **ive**)

Words to Make: is Ed red rid ride side rise dive dives diver drive drives drivers

Part One • Making Words

Have the children arrange their letters in front of their holders to match the pocket-chart letters, with the vowel first and the other letters in alphabetical order. Ask the children to hold up and name each letter, noting the capital letter is used to spell names.

is   "The first word we are going to spell is **is**. Today **is** a sunny day. Everyone say **is**. Use 2 letters to spell **is**."

Choose a child who has **is** spelled correctly to spell **is** with the pocket-chart letters. Have the class chorally spell **is** and fix their word if **is** is not correct.

Ed   "Use 2 letters to spell the name, **Ed**. Do you know anyone named **Ed**? Everyone say **Ed**."

Let a child who has **Ed** spelled correctly with a capital **E** spell **Ed** with the pocket chart letters.

red   "Add a letter to spell **red**. I have a **red** car. Everyone say **red**."

Continue the lesson, giving children explicit instruction about which letters to remove and where to add letters. Put each word in a sentence and have children say each word before making it. Have them "stretch" some words to provide practice for children who are still learning to segment words. Let a child who has spelled the word correctly

make that word with the pocket-chart letters. Choose your struggling readers when the word is an easy word and your advanced readers for harder words. Have the children chorally spell each word after it is made in the pocket chart and fix their word to match.

rid	"Change the vowel to spell **rid**. I cleaned out my closet and got **rid** of a lot of clothes I never wear. Everyone say **rid**."
ride	"Add a letter you don't hear to spell **ride**. I like to **ride** my bike. Everyone say **ride**."
side	"Change the first letter to spell **side**. Which **side** of the gym do you sit on? Everyone say **side**."
rise	"Use 4 letters to spell **rise**. The sun will **rise** in the east. Everyone say **rise**."
dive	"Use 4 letters to spell **dive**. Do you ever **dive** into the pool? Everyone say **dive**."
dives	"Add 1 letter to spell **dives**. Everyone **dives** into the pool. Everyone say **dives**."
diver	"Change 1 letter to spell **diver**. The **diver** rescued the drowning man. Everyone say **diver**."
drive	"Use the same 5 letters to spell **drive**. I **drive** to school every morning. Everyone say **drive**."
drives	"Add 1 letter to spell **drives**. Carl's mom **drives** him to school. Everyone say **drives**."
drivers	**(the secret word)** "It's time for the secret word. I bet everyone can get it today. Add your **r** to **drives** and you will know the secret word."

End the making words part of the lesson by having someone spell **drivers** in the pocket chart and letting everyone hold up their holders to show you **drivers** made in their holders. Have them close the holders and turn their attention to the pocket chart.

Part Two • Sorting Words (Sort for **ed**, **ide**, **ive**, and **ives**)

Tell your students that they are going to say all the words they spelled and then sort the rhyming words. Using the index cards with the words, place them in the pocket chart and have the children pronounce them. Remind them of what they changed to make each word.

"First we used 2 letters to spell **is, i-s**."

"Next we spelled the name, **Ed, E-d**."

"We added the **e** to spell **red, r-e-d**."

"We changed the vowel to spell **rid, r-i-d**."

"We added the **e** to spell **ride, r-i-d-e**."

"We changed the **r** to an **s** to spell **side, s-i-d-e**."

"We used 4 letters to spell **rise, r-i-s-e**."

"We used 4 letters to spell **dive**, **d-i-v-e**."

"We added the **s** to spell **dives**, **d-i-v-e-s**."

"We changed the **s** to an **r** to spell **diver**, **d-i-v-e-r**."

"We moved the letters to spell **drive**, **d-r-i-v-e**."

"We added the **s** to spell **drives**, **d-r-i-v-e-s**."

"We used all our letters to spell the secret word, **drivers**, **d-r-i-v-e-r-s**."

"Now we need to sort out the rhymes. I will take one of each set and you can come and help me find the others."

Arrange one of each set of rhyming words to begin four columns.

red	**ride**	**dive**	**dives**

Choose four children and help them choose the rhyming words and line them up in columns. Have the rhyming words pronounced and have children notice that they all rhyme and they all have the same letters from the vowel to the end of the word.

red	**ride**	**dive**	**dives**
Ed	**side**	**drive**	**drives**

Part Three • Transfer bride hive slide sled

Have the children take out paper. Tell them that you are going to say a word that someone might be writing. By figuring out the rhyming pattern, they will be able to spell the word.

"The first word we are going to spell is **bride**. Kathleen might be writing that her cousin was a beautiful **bride**. Let's all say **bride** and listen for the beginning letters."

Write **br** on an index card when the children decide that **bride** begins with **br**. Take the index card to the pocket chart and have the children pronounce **bride** with each set of rhyming words. When they decide that **bride** rhymes with **ride** and **side**, write **ide** next to **br**. Have the children write **bride** on their papers.

Repeat this procedure for **hive**, **slide**, and **sled**.

Lesson 22

tickets

Letters: | e | i | c | k | s | t | t | (Vowel pattern **ite**)

Make: it tie set sit kit kite site ties skit test sick
tick stick ticket tickets

Sort:

kit	sick	kite
sit	stick	site
it	tick	
skit		

Transfer: bite   quick   quite   brick

Make Words

- Have children name and hold up letters.
- Tell children how many letters to use to make each word.
- Have children say each word and stretch out some words.
- Give sentences to clarify meaning.
- Give specific instructions on how to change words:
  — Add one letter.
  — Change the first letter.
  — Use the same letters.
- Have children clear their holders before making an unrelated word.
- Have children correct their word once it is made in the pocket chart.
- Give children one minute to figure out the secret word and then give them clues.

Sort Words

- Put words in pocket chart in the order made.
- Have children say and spell each word.
- Remind them of how each word was changed to spell the new word.
- Select one word from each rhyming set and line up in columns.
- Let children choose the other words that rhyme.
- Have children pronounce the words.

Transfer Words

- Tell children that they are going to use the rhyming words to spell some new words they might need when they are writing.
- Say the word and a sentence one of your children might write.
- Have children say the word and decide on the beginning letters.
- Write the beginning letters on an index card.
- Take the index card with the beginning letters to the pocket chart and have children say the columns of rhymes and the new word to find the rhyming pattern.
- Write the rhyming pattern on the card to finish the word.
- Have students write the word on paper or a whiteboard.

whisper

Letters: e i h p r s w (Vowel patterns **ipe**, **ise**, and **ire**)

Make: his her sip rip ripe rise wise wipe wire hire ship
whip wipers whisper whisper

Sort:

hire	sip	rise	ripe
wire	rip	wise	wipe
	whip		
	ship		

Transfer: strip stripe fire pipe

Make Words

- Have children name and hold up letters.
- Tell children how many letters to use to make each word.
- Have children say each word and stretch out some words.
- Give sentences to clarify meaning.
- Give specific instructions on how to change words:
  — Add one letter.
  — Change the first letter.
  — Use the same letters.
- Have children clear their holders before making an unrelated word.
- Have children correct their word once it is made in the pocket chart.
- Give children one minute to figure out the secret word and then give them clues.

Sort Words

- Put words in pocket chart in the order made.
- Have children say and spell each word.
- Remind them of how each word was changed to spell the new word.
- Select one word from each rhyming set and line up in columns.
- Let children choose the other words that rhyme.
- Have children pronounce the words.

Transfer Words

- Tell children that they are going to use the rhyming words to spell some new words they might need when they are writing.
- Say the word and a sentence one of your children might write.
- Have children say the word and decide on the beginning letters.
- Write the beginning letters on an index card.
- Take the index card with the beginning letters to the pocket chart and have children say the columns of rhymes and the new word to find the rhyming pattern.
- Write the rhyming pattern on the card to finish the word.
- Have students write the word on paper or a whiteboard.

Lesson 24

sprinkler

Letters: | e | i | k | l | n | p | r | r | s | (Vowel pattern **ine**)

Make: in ink pin pine line like link rink pink sink spin
spine stink sprinkle sprinkler

Sort:

ink	in	pine
link	pin	line
pink	spin	spine
sink		
stink		
rink		

Transfer: shine fin fine wink

Make Words

- Have children name and hold up letters.
- Tell children how many letters to use to make each word.
- Have children say each word and stretch out some words.
- Give sentences to clarify meaning.
- Give specific instructions on how to change words:
  — Add one letter.
  — Change the first letter.
  — Use the same letters.
- Have children clear their holders before making an unrelated word.
- Have children correct their word once it is made in the pocket chart.
- Give children one minute to figure out the secret word and then give them clues.

Sort Words

- Put words in pocket chart in the order made.
- Have children say and spell each word.
- Remind them of how each word was changed to spell the new word.
- Select one word from each rhyming set and line up in columns.
- Let children choose the other words that rhyme.
- Have children pronounce the words.

Transfer Words

- Tell children that they are going to use the rhyming words to spell some new words they might need when they are writing.
- Say the word and a sentence one of your children might write.
- Have children say the word and decide on the beginning letters.
- Write the beginning letters on an index card.
- Take the index card with the beginning letters to the pocket chart and have children say the columns of rhymes and the new word to find the rhyming pattern.
- Write the rhyming pattern on the card to finish the word.
- Have students write the word on paper or a whiteboard.

Lesson 25

crickets

Letters: e i c c k r s t (Vowel patterns **ir**, **ite**, and **ike**)

Make: sit   sir   kit   kite   site   Rick   sick   stir   stick   trick   strike
sticker   crickets

Sort:

sir	sick	kite	kit
stir	trick	site	sit
	stick		
	Rick		

Transfer: thick   quite   quit   bite

Make Words

- Have children name and hold up letters.
- Tell children how many letters to use to make each word.
- Have children say each word and stretch out some words.
- Give sentences to clarify meaning.
- Give specific instructions on how to change words:
  — Add one letter.
  — Change the first letter.
  — Use the same letters.
- Have children clear their holders before making an unrelated word.
- Make sure children use a capital **R** when spelling **Rick**.
- Have children correct their word once it is made in the pocket chart.
- Give children one minute to figure out the secret word and then give them clues.

Sort Words

- Put words in pocket chart in the order made.
- Have children say and spell each word.
- Remind them of how each word was changed to spell the new word.
- Select one word from each rhyming set and line up in columns.
- Let children choose the other words that rhyme.
- Have children pronounce the words.

Transfer Words

- Tell children that they are going to use the rhyming words to spell some new words they might need when they are writing.
- Say the word and a sentence one of your children might write.
- Have children say the word and decide on the beginning letters.
- Write the beginning letters on an index card.
- Take the index card with the beginning letters to the pocket chart and have children say the columns of rhymes and the new word to find the rhyming pattern.
- Write the rhyming pattern on the card to finish the word.
- Have students write the word on paper or a whiteboard.

Lesson 26

stripes

Letters: | e | | i | | p | | r | | s | | s | | t | (Vowel patterns **ir**, **ipe**, and **ies**)

Make: sir sit sip rip ripe site ties pies stir trip strip
sister ripest stripe stripes

Sort:
ties	rip	ripe	sir
pies	trip	stripe	stir
	strip		
	sip		

Transfer: grip gripe flies wipe

Make Words

- Have children name and hold up letters.
- Tell children how many letters to use to make each word.
- Have children say each word and stretch out some words.
- Give sentences to clarify meaning.
- Give specific instructions on how to change words:
  — Add one letter.
  — Change the first letter.
  — Use the same letters.
- Have children clear their holders before making an unrelated word.
- Have children correct their word once it is made in the pocket chart.
- Give children one minute to figure out the secret word and then give them clues.

Sort Words

- Put words in pocket chart in the order made.
- Have children say and spell each word.
- Remind them of how each word was changed to spell the new word.
- Select one word from each rhyming set and line up in columns.
- Let children choose the other words that rhyme.
- Have children pronounce the words.

Transfer Words

- Tell children that they are going to use the rhyming words to spell some new words they might need when they are writing.
- Say the word and a sentence one of your children might write.
- Have children say the word and decide on the beginning letters.
- Write the beginning letters on an index card.
- Take the index card with the beginning letters to the pocket chart and have children say the columns of rhymes and the new word to find the rhyming pattern.
- Write the rhyming pattern on the card to finish the word.
- Have students write the word on paper or a whiteboard.

Lesson 27

spider

Letters: e i d p r s (Vowel patterns **ide, ie,** and **ies**)

Make: Ed red rid rip dip die pie pies dies side ride rise drip pride spider

Sort:

Ed	dip	die	dies	ride
red	drip	pie	pies	pride
	rip			side

Transfer: slide fries bride lie

Make Words

- Have children name and hold up letters.
- Tell children how many letters to use to make each word.
- Have children say each word and stretch out some words.
- Give sentences to clarify meaning.
- Give specific instructions on how to change words:
  — Add one letter.
  — Change the first letter.
  — Use the same letters.
- Have children clear their holders before making an unrelated word.
- Make sure children use a capital **E** when spelling **Ed**.
- Have children correct their word once it is made in the pocket chart.
- Give children one minute to figure out the secret word and then give them clues.

Sort Words

- Put words in pocket chart in the order made.
- Have children say and spell each word.
- Remind them of how each word was changed to spell the new word.
- Select one word from each rhyming set and line up in columns.
- Let children choose the other words that rhyme.
- Have children pronounce the words.

Transfer Words

- Tell children that they are going to use the rhyming words to spell some new words they might need when they are writing.
- Say the word and a sentence one of your children might write.
- Have children say the word and decide on the beginning letters.
- Write the beginning letters on an index card.
- Take the index card with the beginning letters to the pocket chart and have children say the columns of rhymes and the new word to find the rhyming pattern.
- Write the rhyming pattern on the card to finish the word.
- Have students write the word on paper or a whiteboard.

Lesson 28

lightning

Letters: | i | i | g | g | h | l | n | n | t | (Vowel pattern **ight**)

Make: it in tin lit hit hint thin thing night light
lighting lightning

Sort:

in	it	night
tin	lit	light
thin	hit	

Transfer: fight flight bright skit

Make Words

- Have children name and hold up letters.
- Tell children how many letters to use to make each word.
- Have children say each word and stretch out some words.
- Give sentences to clarify meaning.
- Give specific instructions on how to change words:
  — Add one letter.
  — Change the first letter.
  — Use the same letters.
- Have children clear their holders before making an unrelated word.
- Have children correct their word once it is made in the pocket chart.
- Give children one minute to figure out the secret word and then give them clues.

Sort Words

- Put words in pocket chart in the order made.
- Have children say and spell each word.
- Remind them of how each word was changed to spell the new word.
- Select one word from each rhyming set and line up in columns.
- Let children choose the other words that rhyme.
- Have children pronounce the words.

Transfer Words

- Tell children that they are going to use the rhyming words to spell some new words they might need when they are writing.
- Say the word and a sentence one of your children might write.
- Have children say the word and decide on the beginning letters.
- Write the beginning letters on an index card.
- Take the index card with the beginning letters to the pocket chart and have children say the columns of rhymes and the new word to find the rhyming pattern.
- Write the rhyming pattern on the card to finish the word.
- Have students write the word on paper or a whiteboard.

Lesson 29

flashlight

Letters: | a | i | f | g | h | h | l | l | s | t | (Vowel patterns **igh** and **ight**)

Make: sit lit fit fist list fill gill hill high sigh sight light
fight flight flashlight

Sort:

sit	list	sigh	gill	sight
lit	fist	high	fill	light
fit			hill	fight
				flight
				flashlight

Transfer: spill   twist   chill   might

Make Words

- Have children name and hold up letters.
- Tell children how many letters to use to make each word.
- Have children say each word and stretch out some words.
- Give sentences to clarify meaning.
- Give specific instructions on how to change words:
  — Add one letter.
  — Change the first letter.
  — Use the same letters.
- Have children clear their holders before making an unrelated word.
- Have children correct their word once it is made in the pocket chart.
- Give children one minute to figure out the secret word and then give them clues.

Sort Words

- Put words in pocket chart in the order made.
- Have children say and spell each word.
- Remind them of how each word was changed to spell the new word.
- Select one word from each rhyming set and line up in columns.
- Let children choose the other words that rhyme.
- Have children pronounce the words.

Transfer Words

- Tell children that they are going to use the rhyming words to spell some new words they might need when they are writing.
- Say the word and a sentence one of your children might write.
- Have children say the word and decide on the beginning letters.
- Write the beginning letters on an index card.
- Take the index card with the beginning letters to the pocket chart and have children say the columns of rhymes and the new word to find the rhyming pattern.
- Write the rhyming pattern on the card to finish the word.
- Have students write the word on paper or a whiteboard.

Lesson 30

frighten

Letters: | e | i | f | g | h | n | r | t | (Vowel patterns **ire** and **ight**)

Make: her hen ten tin fin fine fire tire thing night right
fight fright fighter frighten

Sort:

fire	tin	night	ten
tire	fin	fight	hen
		fright	frighten
		right	

Transfer: wire might flight spin

Make Words

- Have children name and hold up letters.
- Tell children how many letters to use to make each word.
- Have children say each word and stretch out some words.
- Give sentences to clarify meaning.
- Give specific instructions on how to change words:
  — Add one letter.
  — Change the first letter.
  — Use the same letters.
- Have children clear their holders before making an unrelated word.
- Have children correct their word once it is made in the pocket chart.
- Give children one minute to figure out the secret word and then give them clues.

Sort Words

- Put words in pocket chart in the order made.
- Have children say and spell each word.
- Remind them of how each word was changed to spell the new word.
- Select one word from each rhyming set and line up in columns.
- Let children choose the other words that rhyme.
- Have children pronounce the words.

Transfer Words

- Tell children that they are going to use the rhyming words to spell some new words they might need when they are writing.
- Say the word and a sentence one of your children might write.
- Have children say the word and decide on the beginning letters.
- Write the beginning letters on an index card.
- Take the index card with the beginning letters to the pocket chart and have children say the columns of rhymes and the new word to find the rhyming pattern.
- Write the rhyming pattern on the card to finish the word.
- Have students write the word on paper or a whiteboard.

Tell the children to pretend they are writing and need to spell some words. To spell the word, they should stretch out the word and write the beginning letters and then decide which rhyming words will help them finish writing the word. Remind them that this is exactly what they do in the transfer step of each Making Words lesson but now you want to see if they can do it on their own.

Write these words in columns and have your students chorally pronounce and spell them. Have them notice that each column of words has the same letters from the vowel to the end of the words and that the words in the column rhyme.

light	fine	ride
right	nine	side
night	line	hide

Have the children number a sheet of paper from 1 to 5. Say a word and put it in a sentence. Ask your students to stretch out each word to hear the beginning letters and then decide which words it rhymes with to finish spelling the word:

flight   shine   bride   spine   slight

Record their responses on your record sheet. If students did not use the correct pattern or beginning letters, record what they did use and analyze their errors.

Word	Beginning Letters	Rhyming Pattern
After Lesson 10		
drip	dr	ip
yet	y	et
prop	pr	op
skip	sk	ip
crop	cr	op
After Lesson 20		
thick	th	ick
check	ch	eck
shock	sh	ock
brick	br	ick
clock	cl	ock
After Lesson 30		
flight	fl	ight
shine	sh	ine
bride	br	ide
spine	sp	ine
slight	sl	ight

Lessons 31-40

These 10 lessons teach the common vowel patterns **ai**, **a-e**, **ar**, and **ay** and both sounds for **y**.

Lesson 31

partners

Letters: a e n p r r s t (Patterns **ape** and **ate**)

Words to Make: at ate ape rat rap tap tape trap rate past paste parents partners

Part One • Making Words

Have the children arrange their letters in front of their holders to match the pocket-chart letters, with the vowel first and the other letters in alphabetical order. Ask the children to hold up and name each letter, noting the capital letter is used to spell names.

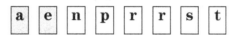

at   "The first word we are going to spell is **at**. The party is **at** my house. Everyone say **at**. Use 2 letters to spell **at**."

Choose a child who has **at** spelled correctly to spell **at** with the pocket-chart letters. Have the class chorally spell **at** and fix their word if **at** is not correct.

ate   "Add a letter you don't hear to spell **ate**. I **ate** all the cookies. Everyone say **ate**."

Let a child who has **ate** spelled correctly spell **ate** with the pocket-chart letters.

ape   "Change 1 letter to spell **ape**. A gorilla is a large **ape**. Everyone say **ape**."

Continue the lesson, giving children explicit instruction about which letters to remove and where to add letters. Put each word in a sentence and have children say each word before making it. Have them "stretch" some words to provide practice for children who are still learning to segment words. Let a child who has spelled the word correctly make that word with the pocket-chart letters. Choose your struggling readers when the word is an easy word and your advanced readers for harder words. Have the children chorally spell each word after it is made in the pocket chart and fix their word to match.

rat	"Use 3 letters to spell **rat**. The **rat** ate the cheese. Everyone say **rat**."
rap	"Change a letter to spell **rap**. Do you like **rap** music? Everyone say **rap**."
tap	"Change the first letter to spell **tap**. Do you know how to **tap** dance? Everyone say **tap**."
tape	"Add a letter to spell **tape**. I will **tape** this on your desk. Everyone say **tape**."
trap	"Use 4 letters to spell **trap**. The mouse was caught in the **trap**. Everyone say **trap**."
rate	"Use 4 letters to spell **rate**. The judge's job is to **rate** the skaters. Everyone say **rate**."
past	"Use 4 letters to spell **past**. I walked **past** the post office. Everyone say **past**."
paste	"Add a letter to spell **paste**. **Paste** your picture on the board. Everyone say **paste**."
parents	"Use 7 letters to spell **parents**. My **parents** came to visit this weekend. Everyone say **parents**."
partners	**(the secret word)** "It's time for the secret word. Signal me if you can figure it out and make it in your holder."

If no one figures out the secret word in one minute, give them a clue.

End the making words part of the lesson by having someone spell **partners** in the pocket chart and letting everyone hold up their holders to show you **partners** made in their holders. Have them close the holders and turn their attention to the pocket chart.

Part Two • Sorting Words (Sort for **ap**, **ape**, and **ate**)

Tell your students that they are going to say all the words they spelled and then sort the rhyming words. Using the index cards with the words, place them in the pocket chart and have the children pronounce them. Remind them of what they changed to make each word.

"First we used 2 letters to spell **at**, **a-t**."

"We added the **e** we don't hear to spell **ate**, **a-t-e**."

"We changed the **t** to a **p** to spell **ape**, **a-p-e**."

"We used 3 letters to spell **rat**, **r-a-t**."

"We changed the last letter to spell **rap**, **r-a-p**."

"We changed the first letter to spell **tap**, **t-a-p**."

"We added the **e** to spell **tape**, **t-a-p-e**."

"We used 4 letters to spell **trap**, **t-r-a-p**."

"We used 4 letters to spell **rate, r-a-t-e**."

"We used 4 letters to spell **past, p-a-s-t**."

"We added the e to spell **paste, p-a-s-t-e**."

"We used 7 letters to spell **parents, p-a-r-e-n-t-s**."

"We used all our letters to spell the secret word, **partners, p-a-r-t-n-e-r-s**."

"Now we need to sort out the rhymes. I will take one of each set and you can come and help me find the others."

Arrange one of each set of rhyming words to begin four columns.

rap	**tape**	**trap**	**ate**

Choose three children and help them choose the rhyming words and line them up in columns. Have the rhyming words pronounced and have children notice that they all rhyme and they all have the same letters from the vowel to the end of the word.

rap	**tape**	**ate**
trap	**ape**	**rate**
tap		

Part Three • Transfer   grape   state   shape   clap

Have the children take out paper. Tell them that you are going to say a word that someone might be writing. By figuring out the rhyming pattern, they will be able to spell the word.

"The first word we are going to spell is **grape**. Terry might be writing that he likes **grape** jelly. Let's all say **grape** and listen for the beginning letters."

Write **gr** on an index card when the children decide that **grape** begins with **gr**. Take the index card to the pocket chart and have the children pronounce **grape** with each set of rhyming words. When they decide that **grape** rhymes with **ape** and **tape**, write **ape** next to **gr**. Have children write **grape** on their papers.

Repeat this procedure for **state, shape,** and **clap**.

Lesson 32

matches

Letters: | a | e | c | h | m | s | t | (Patterns **ace**, **ame**, **are**, and **ate**)

Make: act ace hat mat sat Sam same tame mate hate
race care share shame matches

Sort:

ace	same	mat	care	mate
race	tame	sat	share	hate
	shame	hat		

Transfer: blame skate spare trace

Make Words

- Have children name and hold up letters.
- Tell children how many letters to use to make each word.
- Have children say each word and stretch out some words.
- Give sentences to clarify meaning.
- Give specific instructions on how to change words:
  — Add one letter.
  — Change the first letter.
  — Use the same letters.
- Have children clear their holders before making an unrelated word.
- Make sure children use a capital letter when spelling **Sam**.
- Have children correct their word once it is made in the pocket chart.
- Give children one minute to figure out the secret word and then give them clues.

Sort Words

- Put words in pocket chart in the order made.
- Have children say and spell each word.
- Remind them of how each word was changed to spell the new word.
- Select one word from each rhyming set and line up in columns.
- Let children choose the other words that rhyme.
- Have children pronounce the words.

Transfer Words

- Tell children that they are going to use the rhyming words to spell some new words they might need when they are writing.
- Say the word and a sentence one of your children might write.
- Have children say the word and decide on the beginning letters.
- Write the beginning letters on an index card.
- Take the index card with the beginning letters to the pocket chart and have children say the columns of rhymes and the new word to find the rhyming pattern.
- Write the rhyming pattern on the card to finish the word.
- Have students write the word on paper or a whiteboard.

spinach

Letters: a i c h n p s (Pattern **ain**)

Make: pan pin nip ash cash inch chin chip spin span
pain Spain chain pinch spinach

Sort:

pan	pain	pin	inch	ash	nip
span	chain	chin	pinch	cash	chip
	Spain	spin			

Transfer: brain   smash   trash   slip

Make Words

- Have children name and hold up letters.
- Tell children how many letters to use to make each word.
- Have children say each word and stretch out some words.
- Give sentences to clarify meaning.
- Give specific instructions on how to change words:
  — Add one letter.
  — Change the first letter.
  — Use the same letters.
- Have children clear their holders before making an unrelated word.
- Make sure children use a capital **S** when spelling **Spain**.
- Have children correct their word once it is made in the pocket chart.
- Give children one minute to figure out the secret word and then give them clues.

Sort Words

- Put words in pocket chart in the order made.
- Have children say and spell each word.
- Remind them of how each word was changed to spell the new word.
- Select one word from each rhyming set and line up in columns.
- Let children choose the other words that rhyme.
- Have children pronounce the words.

Transfer Words

- Tell children that they are going to use the rhyming words to spell some new words they might need when they are writing.
- Say the word and a sentence one of your children might write.
- Have children say the word and decide on the beginning letters.
- Write the beginning letters on an index card.
- Take the index card with the beginning letters to the pocket chart and have children say the columns of rhymes and the new word to find the rhyming pattern.
- Write the rhyming pattern on the card to finish the word.
- Have students write the word on paper or a whiteboard.

Lesson 34

principal

Letters: [a] [i] [i] [c] [l] [n] [p] [p] [r]   (Patterns **ail**, **air**, and **ain**)

Make: can   pan   pal   lap   air   pair   pail   nail   rail   rain   clap
plan   pain   plain   principal

Sort:

pail	can	lap	air	rain
rail	pan	clap	pair	pain
nail	plan			plain

Transfer: snail   chair   stain   strap

Make Words

- Have children name and hold up letters.
- Tell children how many letters to use to make each word.
- Have children say each word and stretch out some words.
- Give sentences to clarify meaning.
- Give specific instructions on how to change words:
  — Add one letter.
  — Change the first letter.
  — Use the same letters.
- Have children clear their holders before making an unrelated word.
- Have children correct their word once it is made in the pocket chart.
- Give children one minute to figure out the secret word and then give them clues.

Sort Words

- Put words in pocket chart in the order made.
- Have children say and spell each word.
- Remind them of how each word was changed to spell the new word.
- Select one word from each rhyming set and line up in columns.
- Let children choose the other words that rhyme.
- Have children pronounce the words.

Transfer Words

- Tell children that they are going to use the rhyming words to spell some new words they might need when they are writing.
- Say the word and a sentence one of your children might write.
- Have children say the word and decide on the beginning letters.
- Write the beginning letters on an index card.
- Take the index card with the beginning letters to the pocket chart and have children say the columns of rhymes and the new word to find the rhyming pattern.
- Write the rhyming pattern on the card to finish the word.
- Have students write the word on paper or a whiteboard.

Lesson 35

champion

Letters: | a | i | o | c | h | m | n | p | (Pattern **ain**)

Make: hop   hip   chip   chop   chin   inch   pain   camp   champ
chimp   chain   China   pinch   champion

Sort:

hop	hip	inch	champ	chain
chop	chip	pinch	camp	pain

Transfer: stamp   brain   Spain   flip

Make Words

- Have children name and hold up letters.
- Tell children how many letters to use to make each word.
- Have children say each word and stretch out some words.
- Give sentences to clarify meaning.
- Give specific instructions on how to change words:
  — Add one letter.
  — Change the first letter.
  — Use the same letters.
- Have children clear their holders before making an unrelated word.
- Make sure children use a capital **C** when spelling **China**.
- Have children correct their word once it is made in the pocket chart.
- Give children one minute to figure out the secret word and then give them clues.

Sort Words

- Put words in pocket chart in the order made.
- Have children say and spell each word.
- Remind them of how each word was changed to spell the new word.
- Select one word from each rhyming set and line up in columns.
- Let children choose the other words that rhyme.
- Have children pronounce the words.

Transfer Words

- Tell children that they are going to use the rhyming words to spell some new words they might need when they are writing.
- Say the word and a sentence one of your children might write.
- Have children say the word and decide on the beginning letters.
- Write the beginning letters on an index card.
- Take the index card with the beginning letters to the pocket chart and have children say the columns of rhymes and the new word to find the rhyming pattern.
- Write the rhyming pattern on the card to finish the word.
- Have students write the word on paper or a whiteboard.

Lesson 36

panthers

Letters: | a | e | h | n | p | r | s | t | (Patterns **ate** and **ape**)

Make: at   ate   ape   art   tap   tape   hate   rate   part   path   harp
sharp   sharpen   parents   panthers

Sort:

art	ate	sharp	ape
part	rate	harp	tape
	hate		

Transfer: state   grape   chart   scrape

Make Words

- Have children name and hold up letters.
- Tell children how many letters to use to make each word.
- Have children say each word and stretch out some words.
- Give sentences to clarify meaning.
- Give specific instructions on how to change words:
  — Add one letter.
  — Change the first letter.
  — Use the same letters.
- Have children clear their holders before making an unrelated word.
- Have children correct their word once it is made in the pocket chart.
- Give children one minute to figure out the secret word and then give them clues.

Sort Words

- Put words in pocket chart in the order made.
- Have children say and spell each word.
- Remind them of how each word was changed to spell the new word.
- Select one word from each rhyming set and line up in columns.
- Let children choose the other words that rhyme.
- Have children pronounce the words.

Transfer Words

- Tell children that they are going to use the rhyming words to spell some new words they might need when they are writing.
- Say the word and a sentence one of your children might write.
- Have children say the word and decide on the beginning letters.
- Write the beginning letters on an index card.
- Take the index card with the beginning letters to the pocket chart and have children say the columns of rhymes and the new word to find the rhyming pattern.
- Write the rhyming pattern on the card to finish the word.
- Have students write the word on paper or a whiteboard.

Lesson 37

campfire

Letters: | a | e | i | c | f | m | p | r | (Patterns **ice** and **ace**)

Make: arm car far ice rice race face fire farm camp
ramp cramp price camper campfire

Sort:

farm	ice	face	car	ramp
arm	rice	race	far	camp
	price			cramp

Transfer: slice   space   harm   stamp

Make Words

- Have children name and hold up letters.
- Tell children how many letters to use to make each word.
- Have children say each word and stretch out some words.
- Give sentences to clarify meaning.
- Give specific instructions on how to change words:
  — Add one letter.
  — Change the first letter.
  — Use the same letters.
- Have children clear their holders before making an unrelated word.
- Have children correct their word once it is made in the pocket chart.
- Give children one minute to figure out the secret word and then give them clues.

Sort Words

- Put words in pocket chart in the order made.
- Have children say and spell each word.
- Remind them of how each word was changed to spell the new word.
- Select one word from each rhyming set and line up in columns.
- Let children choose the other words that rhyme.
- Have children pronounce the words.

Transfer Words

- Tell children that they are going to use the rhyming words to spell some new words they might need when they are writing.
- Say the word and a sentence one of your children might write.
- Have children say the word and decide on the beginning letters.
- Write the beginning letters on an index card.
- Take the index card with the beginning letters to the pocket chart and have children say the columns of rhymes and the new word to find the rhyming pattern.
- Write the rhyming pattern on the card to finish the word.
- Have students write the word on paper or a whiteboard.

Lesson 38

driveways

Letters: | a | e | i | d | r | s | v | w | y | (Patterns **ide**, **ise**, and **ives**)

Make: day way say rid ride rise wise wire wide side
sway dives wives drives driveways

Sort:

ride	day	dives	rise
side	say	wives	wise
wide	way	drives	
	sway		

Transfer: stray spray thrives pride

Make Words

- Have children name and hold up letters.
- Tell children how many letters to use to make each word.
- Have children say each word and stretch out some words.
- Give sentences to clarify meaning.
- Give specific instructions on how to change words:
  — Add one letter.
  — Change the first letter.
  — Use the same letters.
- Have children clear their holders before making an unrelated word.
- Have children correct their word once it is made in the pocket chart.
- Give children one minute to figure out the secret words and then give them clues.

Sort Words

- Put words in pocket chart in the order made.
- Have children say and spell each word.
- Remind them of how each word was changed to spell the new word.
- Select one word from each rhyming set and line up in columns.
- Let children choose the other words that rhyme.
- Have children pronounce the words.

Transfer Words

- Tell children that they are going to use the rhyming words to spell some new words they might need when they are writing.
- Say the word and a sentence one of your children might write.
- Have children say the word and decide on the beginning letters.
- Write the beginning letters on an index card.
- Take the index card with the beginning letters to the pocket chart and have children say the columns of rhymes and the new word to find the rhyming pattern.
- Write the rhyming pattern on the card to finish the word.
- Have students write the word on paper or a whiteboard.

Lesson 39

yesterday

Letters: | a | e | e | d | r | s | t | y | y | (Pattern **art** and the two sounds of **y**)

Make: at art sat set yet yes try dry day dart yard stay
tray stray yesterday

Sort:

dry	dart	at	yet	stay
try	art	sat	set	tray
				stray
				day
				yesterday

Transfer: smart   clay   sky   stay

Make Words

- Have children name and hold up letters.
- Tell children how many letters to use to make each word.
- Have children say each word and stretch out some words.
- Give sentences to clarify meaning.
- Give specific instructions on how to change words:
  — Add one letter.
  — Change the first letter.
  — Use the same letters.
- Have children clear their holders before making an unrelated word.
- Have children correct their word once it is made in the pocket chart.
- Give children one minute to figure out the secret word and then give them clues.

Sort Words

- Put words in pocket chart in the order made.
- Have children say and spell each word.
- Remind them of how each word was changed to spell the new word.
- Select one word from each rhyming set and line up in columns.
- Let children choose the other words that rhyme.
- Have children pronounce the words.

Transfer Words

- Tell children that they are going to use the rhyming words to spell some new words they might need when they are writing.
- Say the word and a sentence one of your children might write.
- Have children say the word and decide on the beginning letters.
- Write the beginning letters on an index card.
- Take the index card with the beginning letters to the pocket chart and have children say the columns of rhymes and the new word to find the rhyming pattern.
- Write the rhyming pattern on the card to finish the word.
- Have students write the word on paper or a whiteboard.

Lesson 40

yardstick

Letters: **a** **i** **c** **d** **k** **r** **s** **t** **y** (Pattern **ard** and **y**)

Make: dry cry try sky car card yard dirt dirty stick
trick tricky sticky yardstick

Sort:

card	sticky	cry	stick
yard	tricky	dry	trick
		sky	yardstick
		try	

Transfer: kick hard spy Ricky

Make Words

- Have children name and hold up letters.
- Tell children how many letters to use to make each word.
- Have children say each word and stretch out some words.
- Give sentences to clarify meaning.
- Give specific instructions on how to change words:
  — Add one letter.
  — Change the first letter.
  — Use the same letters.
- Have children clear their holders before making an unrelated word.
- Have children correct their word once it is made in the pocket chart.
- Give children one minute to figure out the secret word and then give them clues.

Sort Words

- Put words in pocket chart in the order made.
- Have children say and spell each word.
- Remind them of how each word was changed to spell the new word.
- Select one word from each rhyming set and line up in columns.
- Let children choose the other words that rhyme.
- Have children pronounce the words.

Transfer Words

- Tell children that they are going to use the rhyming words to spell some new words they might need when they are writing.
- Say the word and a sentence one of your children might write.
- Have children say the word and decide on the beginning letters.
- Write the beginning letters on an index card.
- Take the index card with the beginning letters to the pocket chart and have children say the columns of rhymes and the new word to find the rhyming pattern.
- Write the rhyming pattern on the card to finish the word.
- Have students write the word on paper or a whiteboard.

Assessment Lessons 31-40

Tell the children to pretend they are writing and need to spell some words. To spell the word, they should stretch out the word and write the beginning letters and then decide which rhyming words will help them finish writing the word. Write these words in columns and have your students chorally pronounce and spell them.

rain	date	day
pain	gate	way
train	skate	say

Have the children number a sheet of paper from 1 to 5. Say a word and put it in a sentence. Ask your students to stretch out each word to hear the beginning letters and then decide which words it rhymes with to finish spelling the word:

plate   stray   grain   spray   chain

Record their responses on your record sheet. If students did not use the correct pattern or beginning letters, record what they did use and analyze their errors.

Word	Beginning Letters	Rhyming Pattern
After Lesson 10		
drip	dr	ip
yet	y	et
prop	pr	op
skip	sk	ip
crop	cr	op
After Lesson 20		
thick	th	ick
check	ch	eck
shock	sh	ock
brick	br	ick
clock	cl	ock

Word	Beginning Letters	Rhyming Pattern
After Lesson 30		
flight	fl	ight
shine	sh	ine
bride	br	ide
spine	sp	ine
slight	sl	ight
After Lesson 40		
plate	pl	ate
stray	str	ay
grain	gr	ain
spray	spr	ay
chain	ch	ain

Lessons 41-50

These 10 lessons teach the common vowel patterns **ee**, **ea**, and **er**.

Lesson 41

experts

Letters: e e p r s t x   (Patterns **ee** and **eep**)

Words to Make: pet set see Rex rest pest step tree seep
steep steer Peter pester experts

Part One • Making Words

 Have the children arrange their letters in front of their holders to match the pocket-chart letters, with the vowel first and the other letters in alphabetical order. Ask the children to hold up and name each letter, noting the capital letter is used to spell names.

pet   "The first word we are going to spell is **pet**. Do you have a pet? Everyone say **pet**. Use 3 letters to spell **pet**."

Choose a child who has **pet** spelled correctly to spell **pet** with the pocket-chart letters. Have the class chorally spell **pet** and fix their word if **pet** is not correct.

set   "Change the first letter to spell **set**. Please **set** the table. Everyone say **set**."

Let a child who has **set** spelled correctly spell **set** with the pocket-chart letters. .

see   "Change 1 letter to spell **see**. I **see** all my smart students. Everyone say **see**."

Continue the lesson, giving children explicit instruction about which letters to remove and where to add letters. Put each word in a sentence and have children say each word before making it. Have them "stretch" some words to provide practice for children who are still learning to segment words. Let a child who has spelled the word correctly

make that word with the pocket-chart letters. Choose your struggling readers when the word is an easy word and your advanced readers for harder words. Have the children chorally spell each word after it is made in the pocket chart and fix their word to match.

Rex	"Use 3 letters to spell the name **Rex**. **Rex** is my neighbor's dog. Everyone say **Rex**."
rest	"Use 4 letters to spell **rest**. Who ate the **rest** of the cookies? Everyone say **rest**."
pest	"Change the first letter to spell **pest**. Don't be a **pest**. Everyone say **pest**."
step	"Use the same letters to spell **step**. Do not **step** on the ants. Everyone say **step**."
tree	"Use 4 letters to spell **tree**. We planted a **tree**. Everyone say **tree**."
seep	"Use 4 letters to spell **seep**. When it rains hard, the water might **seep** under the door. Everyone say **seep**."
steep	"Add 1 letter to spell **steep**. We climbed a **steep** hill. Everyone say **steep**."
steer	"Change 1 letter to spell **steer**. When you drive, you have to **steer** the car. Everyone say **steer**."
Peter	"Use 5 letters to spell the name **Peter**. I have a cousin named **Peter**. Everyone say **Peter**."
pester	"Add a letter to spell **pester**. Please don't **pester** me. Everyone say **pester**."
experts	**(the secret word)** "It's time for the secret word. Signal me if you can figure it out and make it in your holder."

If no one figures out the secret word in one minute, give them a clue.

End the making words part of the lesson by having someone spell **experts** in the pocket chart and letting everyone hold up their holders to show you **experts** made in their holders. Have them close the holders and turn their attention to the pocket chart.

Part Two • Sorting Words (Sort for **et**, **est**, **ee**, and **eep**)

Tell your students that they are going to say all the words they spelled and then sort the rhyming words. Using the index cards with the words, place them in the pocket chart and have the children pronounce them. Remind them of what they changed to make each word.

"First we used 3 letters to spell **pet**, **p-e-t**."

"We changed the first letter to spell **set**, **s-e-t**."

"We changed the last letter to spell **see**, **s-e-e**."

"We used 3 letters to spell the name **Rex**, **R-e-x**."

"We changed the last letter to spell **rest**, **r-e-s-t**."

"We changed the first letter to spell **pest**, **p-e-s-t**."

"We used the same letters to spell **step, s-t-e-p**."

"We used 4 letters to spell **tree, t-r-e-e**."

"We used 4 letters to spell **seep, s-e-e-p**."

"We added a letter to spell **steep, s-t-e-e-p**."

"We changed the last letter to spell **steer, s-t-e-e-r**."

"We used 5 letters to spell the name **Peter, P-e-t-e-r**."

"We added a letter to spell **pester, p-e-s-t-e-r**."

"We used all our letters to spell the secret word, **experts, e-x-p-e-r-t-s**."

"Now we need to sort out the rhymes. I will take one of each set and you can come and help me find the others."

Arrange one of each set of rhyming words to begin four columns.

pet	pest	tree	seep

Choose four children and help them choose the rhyming words and line them up in columns. Have the rhyming words pronounced and have children notice that they all rhyme and they all have the same letters from the vowel to the end of the word.

pet	pest	tree	seep
set	rest	see	steep

Part Three • Transfer jeep sheep beep sweep

Have the children take out paper. Tell them that you are going to say a word that someone might be writing. By figuring out the rhyming pattern, they will be able to spell the word.

"The first word we are going to spell is **jeep**. Kevin might be writing that he would like to drive a **jeep**. Let's all say **jeep** and listen for the beginning letters."

Write **j** on an index card when the children decide that **jeep** begins with **j**. Take the index card to the pocket chart and have the children pronounce **jeep** with each set of rhyming words. When they decide that **jeep** rhymes with **seep** and **sweep**, write **eep** next to **j**. Have children write **jeep** on their papers.

Repeat this procedure for **sheep**, **beep**, and **sweep**.

Lesson 42

September

Letters: | e | e | e | b | m | p | r | s | t | (Patterns **ee** and **eep**)

Make: see set pet pest rest best beep seep steep beets
meets Peter pester temper September

Sort:

beep	rest	set	beets
seep	best	pet	meets
steep	pest		

Transfer: creep sheets west sleep

Make Words

- Have children name and hold up letters.
- Tell children how many letters to use to make each word.
- Have children say each word and stretch out some words.
- Give sentences to clarify meaning.
- Give specific instructions on how to change words:
  — Add one letter.
  — Change the first letter.
  — Use the same letters.
- Have children clear their holders before making an unrelated word.
- Make sure children use a capital letter when spelling **Peter** and **September**.
- Have children correct their word once it is made in the pocket chart.
- Give children one minute to figure out the secret word and then give them clues.

Sort Words

- Put words in pocket chart in the order made.
- Have children say and spell each word.
- Remind them of how each word was changed to spell the new word.
- Select one word from each rhyming set and line up in columns.
- Let children choose the other words that rhyme.
- Have children pronounce the words.

Transfer Words

- Tell children that they are going to use the rhyming words to spell some new words they might need when they are writing.
- Say the word and a sentence one of your children might write.
- Have children say the word and decide on the beginning letters.
- Write the beginning letters on an index card.
- Take the index card with the beginning letters to the pocket chart and have children say the columns of rhymes and the new word to find the rhyming pattern.
- Write the rhyming pattern on the card to finish the word.
- Have students write the word on paper or a whiteboard.

Lesson 43

different

Letters: | e | e | i | d | f | f | n | r | t | (Patterns **ee** and **eed**)

Make: Ed   fed   fee   Ned   den   ten   teen   need   feed   free   tender   fender   fifteen   different

Sort:

ed	need	den	fee	tender
fed	feed	ten	free	fender
Ned				

Transfer: speed   blender   spree   then

Make Words

- Have children name and hold up letters.
- Tell children how many letters to use to make each word.
- Have children say each word and stretch out some words.
- Give sentences to clarify meaning.
- Give specific instructions on how to change words:
  — Add one letter.
  — Change the first letter.
  — Use the same letters.
- Have children clear their holders before making an unrelated word.
- Make sure children use capital letters when spelling names.
- Have children correct their word once it is made in the pocket chart.
- Give children one minute to figure out the secret word and then give them clues.

Sort Words

- Put words in pocket chart in the order made.
- Have children say and spell each word.
- Remind them of how each word was changed to spell the new word.
- Select one word from each rhyming set and line up in columns.
- Let children choose the other words that rhyme.
- Have children pronounce the words.

Transfer Words

- Tell children that they are going to use the rhyming words to spell some new words they might need when they are writing.
- Say the word and a sentence one of your children might write.
- Have children say the word and decide on the beginning letters.
- Write the beginning letters on an index card.
- Take the index card with the beginning letters to the pocket chart and have children say the columns of rhymes and the new word to find the rhyming pattern.
- Write the rhyming pattern on the card to finish the word.
- Have students write the word on paper or a whiteboard.

Lesson 44

treats

Letters: | a | e | r | s | t | t | (Patterns **ea** and **eat**)

Make: at art rat ate eat tea sea seat east rate state taste treat treats

Sort:

ate	sea	seat
rate	tea	treat
state		eat

Transfer: cheat   crate   neat   flea

Make Words

- Have children name and hold up letters.
- Tell children how many letters to use to make each word.
- Have children say each word and stretch out some words.
- Give sentences to clarify meaning.
- Give specific instructions on how to change words:
  — Add one letter.
  — Change the first letter.
  — Use the same letters.
- Have children clear their holders before making an unrelated word.
- Have children correct their word once it is made in the pocket chart.
- Give children one minute to figure out the secret word and then give them clues.

Sort Words

- Put words in pocket chart in the order made.
- Have children say and spell each word.
- Remind them of how each word was changed to spell the new word.
- Select one word from each rhyming set and line up in columns.
- Let children choose the other words that rhyme.
- Have children pronounce the words.

Transfer Words

- Tell children that they are going to use the rhyming words to spell some new words they might need when they are writing.
- Say the word and a sentence one of your children might write.
- Have children say the word and decide on the beginning letters.
- Write the beginning letters on an index card.
- Take the index card with the beginning letters to the pocket chart and have children say the columns of rhymes and the new word to find the rhyming pattern.
- Write the rhyming pattern on the card to finish the word.
- Have students write the word on paper or a whiteboard.

Lesson 45

skater

Letters: | a | e | k | r | s | t | (Pattern eat)

Make: at ate eat rat sat set seat east rate rake take
Kate skate skater

Sort:

ate	rake	sat	eat
rate	take	rat	seat
Kate		at	
skate			

Transfer: treat   snake   cheat   plate

Make Words

- Have children name and hold up letters.
- Tell children how many letters to use to make each word.
- Have children say each word and stretch out some words.
- Give sentences to clarify meaning.
- Give specific instructions on how to change words:
    — Add one letter.
    — Change the first letter.
    — Use the same letters.
- Have children clear their holders before making an unrelated word.
- Make sure children use a capital **K** when spelling **Kate**.
- Have children correct their word once it is made in the pocket chart.
- Give children one minute to figure out the secret word and then give them clues.

Sort Words

- Put words in pocket chart in the order made.
- Have children say and spell each word.
- Remind them of how each word was changed to spell the new word.
- Select one word from each rhyming set and line up in columns.
- Let children choose the other words that rhyme.
- Have children pronounce the words.

Transfer Words

- Tell children that they are going to use the rhyming words to spell some new words they might need when they are writing.
- Say the word and a sentence one of your children might write.
- Have children say the word and decide on the beginning letters.
- Write the beginning letters on an index card.
- Take the index card with the beginning letters to the pocket chart and have children say the columns of rhymes and the new word to find the rhyming pattern.
- Write the rhyming pattern on the card to finish the word.
- Have students write the word on paper or a whiteboard.

Lesson 46

tables/stable

Letters: | a | e | b | l | s | t | (Patterns **eat**, **east**, and **eal**)

This lesson has two secret words: **tables** and **stable**.

Make: let set bet best beat seat seal east last blast
beast least steal tables stable

Sort:

seat	bet	last	east	seal
beat	set	blast	beast	steal
	let		least	

Transfer: feast   deal   cast   cheat

Make Words

- Have children name and hold up letters.
- Tell children how many letters to use to make each word.
- Have children say each word and stretch out some words.
- Give sentences to clarify meaning.
- Give specific instructions on how to change words:
  — Add one letter.
  — Change the first letter.
  — Use the same letters.
- Have children clear their holders before making an unrelated word.
- Have children correct their word once it is made in the pocket chart.
- Give children one minute to figure out the secret words and then give them clues.

Sort Words

- Put words in pocket chart in the order made.
- Have children say and spell each word.
- Remind them of how each word was changed to spell the new word.
- Select one word from each rhyming set and line up in columns.
- Let children choose the other words that rhyme.
- Have children pronounce the words.

Transfer Words

- Tell children that they are going to use the rhyming words to spell some new words they might need when they are writing.
- Say the word and a sentence one of your children might write.
- Have children say the word and decide on the beginning letters.
- Write the beginning letters on an index card.
- Take the index card with the beginning letters to the pocket chart and have children say the columns of rhymes and the new word to find the rhyming pattern.
- Write the rhyming pattern on the card to finish the word.
- Have students write the word on paper or a whiteboard.

Lesson 47

smartest

Letters: | a | e | m | r | s | s | t | t | (Patterns **eam** and **eat**)

Make: arm art eat ate mate meat team tame same smart
treat state steam stream smartest

Sort:

tame	eat	state	team
same	meat	ate	steam
	treat	mate	stream

Transfer: cream   dream   scream   flame

Make Words

- Have children name and hold up letters.
- Tell children how many letters to use to make each word.
- Have children say each word and stretch out some words.
- Give sentences to clarify meaning.
- Give specific instructions on how to change words:
  — Add one letter.
  — Change the first letter.
  — Use the same letters.
- Have children clear their holders before making an unrelated word.
- Have children correct their word once it is made in the pocket chart.
- Give children one minute to figure out the secret word and then give them clues.

Sort Words

- Put words in pocket chart in the order made.
- Have children say and spell each word.
- Remind them of how each word was changed to spell the new word.
- Select one word from each rhyming set and line up in columns.
- Let children choose the other words that rhyme.
- Have children pronounce the words.

Transfer Words

- Tell children that they are going to use the rhyming words to spell some new words they might need when they are writing.
- Say the word and a sentence one of your children might write.
- Have children say the word and decide on the beginning letters.
- Write the beginning letters on an index card.
- Take the index card with the beginning letters to the pocket chart and have children say the columns of rhymes and the new word to find the rhyming pattern.
- Write the rhyming pattern on the card to finish the word.
- Have students write the word on paper or a whiteboard.

Lesson 48

teaching/cheating

Letters: | a | e | i | c | g | h | n | t | (Patterns **ice**, **eat**, and **each**)

This lesson has two secret words: **teaching** and **cheating**.

Make: act cat hat ice nice hate heat neat each teach cheat acting heating teaching cheating

Sort:

ice	each	hat	eat	heating
nice	teach	cat	heat	cheating
			neat	
			cheat	

Transfer: peach   beating   beach   seat

Make Words

- Have children name and hold up letters.
- Tell children how many letters to use to make each word.
- Have children say each word and stretch out some words.
- Give sentences to clarify meaning.
- Give specific instructions on how to change words:
  — Add one letter.
  — Change the first letter.
  — Use the same letters.
- Have children clear their holders before making an unrelated word.
- Have children correct their word once it is made in the pocket chart.
- Give children one minute to figure out the secret words and then give them clues.

Sort Words

- Put words in pocket chart in the order made.
- Have children say and spell each word.
- Remind them of how each word was changed to spell the new word.
- Select one word from each rhyming set and line up in columns.
- Let children choose the other words that rhyme.
- Have children pronounce the words.

Transfer Words

- Tell children that they are going to use the rhyming words to spell some new words they might need when they are writing.
- Say the word and a sentence one of your children might write.
- Have children say the word and decide on the beginning letters.
- Write the beginning letters on an index card.
- Take the index card with the beginning letters to the pocket chart and have children say the columns of rhymes and the new word to find the rhyming pattern.
- Write the rhyming pattern on the card to finish the word.
- Have students write the word on paper or a whiteboard.

Lesson 49

classmate

Letters: | a | a | e | c | l | m | s | s | t | (Patterns **eam** and **eat**)

Make: at   ate   eat   mat   met   set   seat   meat   mate   tame   team
steam   class   cleats   classmate

Sort:

ate	team	seat	set	at
mate	steam	meat	met	mat
classmate		eat		

Transfer: stream   cream   beat   dream

Make Words

- Have children name and hold up letters.
- Tell children how many letters to use to make each word.
- Have children say each word and stretch out some words.
- Give sentences to clarify meaning.
- Give specific instructions on how to change words:
  — Add one letter.
  — Change the first letter.
  — Use the same letters.
- Have children clear their holders before making an unrelated word.
- Have children correct their word once it is made in the pocket chart.
- Give children one minute to figure out the secret word and then give them clues.

Sort Words

- Put words in pocket chart in the order made.
- Have children say and spell each word.
- Remind them of how each word was changed to spell the new word.
- Select one word from each rhyming set and line up in columns.
- Let children choose the other words that rhyme.
- Have children pronounce the words.

Transfer Words

- Tell children that they are going to use the rhyming words to spell some new words they might need when they are writing.
- Say the word and a sentence one of your children might write.
- Have children say the word and decide on the beginning letters.
- Write the beginning letters on an index card.
- Take the index card with the beginning letters to the pocket chart and have children say the columns of rhymes and the new word to find the rhyming pattern.
- Write the rhyming pattern on the card to finish the word.
- Have students write the word on paper or a whiteboard.

Lesson 50

cheaters/teachers

Letters: `a` `e` `e` `c` `h` `r` `s` `t` (Patterns **eat** and **each**)

This lesson has two secret words: **cheaters** and **teachers**.

Make: at ate eat sat hat heat seat east each teach
cheat cheats cheaters teachers

Sort:

each	seat	at	eaters
teach	cheat	hat	cheaters
	eat	sat	
	heat		

Transfer: beach peach preach beat

Make Words

- Have children name and hold up letters.
- Tell children how many letters to use to make each word.
- Have children say each word and stretch out some words.
- Give sentences to clarify meaning.
- Give specific instructions on how to change words:
  — Add one letter.
  — Change the first letter.
  — Use the same letters.
- Have children clear their holders before making an unrelated word.
- Have children correct their word once it is made in the pocket chart.
- Tell students that there are two secret words today. Give children one minute to figure out the secret words and then give them clues.

Sort Words

- Put words in pocket chart in the order made.
- Have children say and spell each word.
- Remind them of how each word was changed to spell the new word.
- Select one word from each rhyming set and line up in columns.
- Let children choose the other words that rhyme.
- Have children pronounce the words.

Transfer Words

- Tell the children that they are going to use the rhyming words to spell some new words they might need when they are writing.
- Say word and a sentence one of your children might write.
- Have children say the word and decide on the beginning letters.
- Write the beginning letters on an index card.
- Take the index card with the beginning letters to the pocket chart and have children say the columns of rhymes and the new word to find the rhyming pattern.
- Write the rhyming pattern on the card to finish the word.
- Have students write the word on paper or a whiteboard.

Assessment Lessons 41-50

Tell the children to pretend they are writing and need to spell some words. To spell the word, they should stretch out the word and write the beginning letters and then decide which rhyming words will help them finish writing the word. Write these words in columns and have your students chorally pronounce and spell them.

team	need	game
steam	feed	came
dream	seed	name

Have the children number a sheet of paper from 1 to 5. Say a word and put it in a sentence. Ask your students to use the rhyming words to spell each word.

bleed   shame   scream   greed   stream

Record their responses on your record sheet. If students did not use the correct pattern or beginning letters, record what they did use and analyze their errors.

Word	Beginning Letters	Rhyming Pattern
After Lesson 10		
drip	dr	ip
yet	y	et
prop	pr	op
skip	sk	ip
crop	cr	op
After Lesson 20		
thick	th	ick
check	ch	eck
shock	sh	ock
brick	br	ick
clock	cl	ock
After Lesson 30		
flight	fl	ight
shine	sh	ine
bride	br	ide
spine	sp	ine
slight	sl	ight

Word	Beginning Letters	Rhyming Pattern
After Lesson 40		
plate	pl	ate
stray	str	ay
grain	gr	ain
spray	spr	ay
chain	ch	ain
After Lesson 50		
bleed	bl	eed
shame	sh	ame
scream	scr	eam
greed	gr	eed
stream	str	eam

Lessons 51-60

These 10 lessons teach the common vowel patterns **u**, **ue**, **u-e**, and **ur**.

Lesson 51

buckets

Letters: e u b c k s t (Patterns **ub** and **ube**)

Words to Make: us bus but cut tub sub cub cube tube cute
bust buck tuck stuck buckets

Part One • Making Words

Have the children arrange their letters in front of their holders to match the pocket-chart letters, with the vowel first and the other letters in alphabetical order. Ask the children to hold up and name each letter, noting the capital letter is used to spell names.

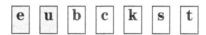

us   "The first word we are going to spell is **us**. Look at **us**! Everyone say **us**. Use 2 letters to spell **us**."

Choose a child who has **us** spelled correctly to spell **us** with the pocket-chart letters. Have the class chorally spell **us** and fix their word if **us** is not correct.

bus   "Add a letter to spell **bus**. Did you ride the **bus**? Everyone say **bus**."

Let a child who has **bus** spelled correctly spell **bus** with the pocket-chart letters.

but   "Change 1 letter to spell **but**. We wanted to go outside **but** is was raining. Everyone say **but**."

Continue the lesson, giving children explicit instruction about which letters to re-move and where to add letters. Put each word in a sentence and have children say each word before making it. Have them "stretch" some words to provide practice for children who are still learning to segment words. Let a child who has spelled the word correctly

make that word with the pocket-chart letters. Choose your struggling readers when the word is an easy word and your advanced readers for harder words. Have the children chorally spell each word after it is made in the pocket chart and fix their word to match.

cut	"Change 1 letter to spell **cut**. I **cut** my finger. Everyone say **cut**."
tub	"Use 3 letters to spell **tub**. I washed my dog in the **tub**. Everyone say **tub**."
sub	"Change the first letter to spell **sub**. When our teacher is out, we have a **sub**. Everyone say **sub**."
cub	"Change 1 letter to spell **cub**. A baby bear is a **cub**. Everyone say **cub**."
cube	"Add a letter to spell **cube**. I put an ice **cube** in my soda. Everyone say **cube**."
tube	"Change a letter to spell **tube**. Toothpaste comes in a **tube**. Everyone say **tube**."
cute	"Use 4 letters to spell **cute**. That puppy is so **cute**. Everyone say **cute**."
bust	"Use 4 letters to spell **bust**. Did the balloon **bust**? Everyone say **bust**."
buck	"Change 2 letters to spell the name **buck**. A male deer is called a **buck**. Everyone say **buck**."
tuck	"Change a letter to spell **tuck**. Please **tuck** your shirt in. Everyone say **tuck**."
stuck	"Add a letter to spell **stuck**. The car was **stuck** in the mud. Everyone say **stuck**."
buckets	**(the secret word)** "It's time for the secret word. Signal me if you can figure it out and make it in your holder."

If no one figures out the secret word in one minute, give them a clue.

End the making words part of the lesson by having someone spell **buckets** in the pocket chart and letting everyone hold up their holders to show you **buckets** made in their holders. Have them close the holders and turn their attention to the pocket chart.

Part Two • Sorting Words (Sort for **us**, **ut**, **ub**, **ube**, and **uck**)

Tell your students that they are going to say all the words they spelled and then sort the rhyming words. Using the index cards with the words, place them in the pocket chart and have the children pronounce them. Remind them of what they changed to make each word.

"First we used 2 letters to spell **us**, u-s."

"We added a letter to spell **bus**, b-u-s."

"We changed the last letter to spell **but**, b-u-t."

"We changed the first letter to spell **cut**, c-u-t."

"We used 3 letters to spell **tub**, t-u-b."

"We changed the first letter to spell **sub, s-u-b**."

"We changed the first letter again to spell **cub, c-u-b**."

"We added the **e** to spell **cube, c-u-b-e**."

"We changed the first letter to spell **tube, t-u-b-e**."

"We used 4 letters to spell **cute, c-u-t-e**."

"We used 4 letters to spell **bust, b-u-s-t**."

"We changed the last 2 letters to spell **buck, b-u-c-k**."

"We changed the first letter to spell **tuck, t-u-c-k**."

"We added a letter to spell **stuck, s-t-u-c-k**."

"We used all our letters to spell the secret word, **buckets, b-u-c-k-e-t-s**."

"Now we need to sort out the rhymes. I will take one of each set and you can come and help me find the others."

Arrange one of each set of rhyming words to begin five columns.

us	but	tub	tube	stuck

Choose five children and help them choose the rhyming words and line them up in columns. Have the rhyming words pronounced and have children notice that they all rhyme and they all have the same letters from the vowel to the end of the word.

us	but	tub	tube	stuck
bus	cut	sub	cube	tuck
		cub		buck

Part Three • Transfer truck club scrub

Have the children take out paper. Tell them that you are going to say a word that someone might be writing. By figuring out the rhyming pattern, they will be able to spell the word.

"The first word we are going to spell is **truck**. Paulo might be writing that his uncle is a **truck** driver. Let's all say **truck** and listen for the beginning letters."

Write **tr** on an index card when the children decide that **truck** begins with **tr**. Take the index card to the pocket chart and have the children pronounce **truck** with each set of rhyming words. When they decide that **truck** rhymes with **buck, tuck,** and **stuck,** write **uck** next to **tr**. Have children write **truck** on their papers.

Repeat this procedure for **club** and **scrub**.

Lesson 52

jugglers

Letters: e u g g j l r s (Patterns **ue**, **us**, and **use**)

Make: us   Gus   use   Sue   leg   lug   rug   jug   slug   glue   rule
sure   juggle   jugglers

Sort:

Gus	Sue	jug
us	glue	rug
		lug
		slug

Transfer: clue   plug   true   bus

Make Words

- Have children name and hold up letters.
- Tell children how many letters to use to make each word.
- Have children say each word and stretch out some words.
- Give sentences to clarify meaning.
- Give specific instructions on how to change words:
  — Add one letter.
  — Change the first letter.
  — Use the same letters.
- Have children clear their holders before making an unrelated word.
- Make sure children use a capital letter when spelling **Gus** and **Sue**.
- Have children correct their word once it is made in the pocket chart.
- Give children one minute to figure out the secret word and then give them clues.

Sort Words

- Put words in pocket chart in the order made.
- Have children say and spell each word.
- Remind them of how each word was changed to spell the new word.
- Select one word from each rhyming set and line up in columns.
- Let children choose the other words that rhyme.
- Have children pronounce the words.

Transfer Words

- Tell children that they are going to use the rhyming words to spell some new words they might need when they are writing.
- Say the word and a sentence one of your children might write.
- Have children say the word and decide on the beginning letters.
- Write the beginning letters on an index card.
- Take the index card with the beginning letters to the pocket chart and have children say the columns of rhymes and the new word to find the rhyming pattern.
- Write the rhyming pattern on the card to finish the word.
- Have students write the word on paper or a whiteboard.

Lesson 53

bumblebees

Letters: `e` `e` `e` `u` `b` `b` `b` `l` `m` `s` (Patterns **us**, **um**, and **ue**)

Make: us bus sub Sue use bee see seem sum slum blue
bees bulbs bubbles bumblebees

Sort:

bus	sum	Sue	bee
us	slum	blue	see

Transfer: free   true   plum   glee

Make Words

- Have children name and hold up letters.
- Tell children how many letters to use to make each word.
- Have children say each word and stretch out some words.
- Give sentences to clarify meaning.
- Give specific instructions on how to change words:
  — Add one letter.
  — Change the first letter.
  — Use the same letters.
- Have children clear their holders before making an unrelated word.
- Make sure children use capital letters when spelling names.
- Have children correct their word once it is made in the pocket chart.
- Give children one minute to figure out the secret word and then give them clues.

Sort Words

- Put words in pocket chart in the order made.
- Have children say and spell each word.
- Remind them of how each word was changed to spell new word.
- Select one word from each rhyming set and line up in columns.
- Let children choose the other words that rhyme.
- Have children pronounce the words.

Transfer Words

- Tell children that they are going to use the rhyming words to spell some new words they might need when they are writing.
- Say the word and a sentence one of your children might write.
- Have children say the word and decide on the beginning letters.
- Write the beginning letters on an index card.
- Take the index card with the beginning letters to the pocket chart and have children say the columns of rhymes and the new word to find the rhyming pattern.
- Write the rhyming pattern on the card to finish the word.
- Have students write the word on paper or a whiteboard.

Lesson 54

umbrellas

Letters: | a | e | u | b | l | l | m | r | s | (Patterns **us**, **ue**, **ule**, and **ure**)

Make: us   bus   use   Sue   sure   lure   rule   mule   blue   blur
mural   amuse   lumber   umbrellas

Sort:

us	lure	rule	Sue
bus	sure	mule	blue

Transfer: cure   plus   pure   due

Make Words

- Have children name and hold up letters.
- Tell children how many letters to use to make each word.
- Have children say each word and stretch out some words.
- Give sentences to clarify meaning.
- Give specific instructions on how to change words:
  — Add one letter.
  — Change the first letter.
  — Use the same letters.
- Have children clear their holders before making an unrelated word.
- Have children correct their word once it is made in the pocket chart.
- Give children one minute to figure out the secret word and then give them clues.

Sort Words

- Put words in pocket chart in the order made.
- Have children say and spell each word.
- Remind them of how each word was changed to spell the new word.
- Select one word from each rhyming set and line up in columns.
- Let children choose the other words that rhyme.
- Have children pronounce the words.

Transfer Words

- Tell children that they are going to use the rhyming words to spell some new words they might need when they are writing.
- Say the word and a sentence one of your children might write.
- Have children say the word and decide on the beginning letters.
- Write the beginning letters on an index card.
- Take the index card with the beginning letters to the pocket chart and have children say the columns of rhymes and the new word to find the rhyming pattern.
- Write the rhyming pattern on the card to finish the word.
- Have students write the word on paper or a whiteboard.

Lesson 55

picture

Letters: | e | | i | | u | | c | | p | | r | | t | (Patterns **up**, **ue**, and **ure**)

Make: up cup cut cue pie tie ice rice ripe cute cure
pure true price picture

Sort:

ice	up	tie	pure	true
rice	cup	pie	cure	cue
price			picture	

Transfer: twice   clue   lure   sure

Make Words

- Have children name and hold up letters.
- Tell children how many letters to use to make each word.
- Have children say each word and stretch out some words.
- Give sentences to clarify meaning.
- Give specific instructions on how to change words:
  — Add one letter.
  — Change the first letter.
  — Use the same letters.
- Have children clear their holders before making an unrelated word.
- Make sure children use a capital **S** when spelling **Sue**.
- Have children correct their word once it is made in the pocket chart.
- Give children one minute to figure out the secret word and then give them clues.

Sort Words

- Put words in pocket chart in the order made.
- Have children say and spell each word.
- Remind them of how each word was changed to spell the new word.
- Select one word from each rhyming set and line up in columns.
- Let children choose the other words that rhyme.
- Have children pronounce the words.

Transfer Words

- Tell children that they are going to use the rhyming words to spell some new words they might need when they are writing.
- Say the word and a sentence one of your children might write.
- Have children say the word and decide on the beginning letters.
- Write the beginning letters on an index card.
- Take the index card with the beginning letters to the pocket chart and have children say the columns of rhymes and the new word to find the rhyming pattern.
- Write the rhyming pattern on the card to finish the word.
- Have students write the word on paper or a whiteboard.

Lesson 56

furniture

Letters: | e | i | u | u | f | n | r | r | t | (Patterns **un** and **ur**)

Make: tie fun fur run runt turn turf true tire fire
untie untrue return future furniture

Sort:
fire	fun
tire	run

Transfer: wire   stun   hire   bun

Make Words

- Have children name and hold up letters.
- Tell children how many letters to use to make each word.
- Have children say each word and stretch out some words.
- Give sentences to clarify meaning.
- Give specific instructions on how to change words:
  — Add one letter.
  — Change the first letter.
  — Use the same letters.
- Have children clear their holders before making an unrelated word.
- Have children correct their word once it is made in the pocket chart.
- Give children one minute to figure out the secret word and then give them clues.

Sort Words

- Put words in pocket chart in the order made.
- Have children say and spell each word.
- Remind them of how each word was changed to spell the new word.
- Select one word from each rhyming set and line up in columns.
- Let children choose the other words that rhyme.
- Have children pronounce the words.

Transfer Words

- Tell children that they are going to use the rhyming words to spell some new words they might need when they are writing.
- Say the word and a sentence one of your children might write.
- Have children say the word and decide on the beginning letters.
- Write the beginning letters on an index card.
- Take the index card with the beginning letters to the pocket chart and have children say the columns of rhymes and the new word to find the rhyming pattern.
- Write the rhyming pattern on the card to finish the word.
- Have students write the word on paper or a whiteboard.

Lesson 57

ambulance

Letters: a a e u b c l m n (Patterns **ub** and **ue**)

Make: an can man ban bun cub cue clue blue cube club mule uncle ambulance

Sort:

can	cue	cub
an	clue	club
man	blue	
ban		

Transfer: true   plan   glue   snub

Make Words

- Have children name and hold up letters.
- Tell children how many letters to use to make each word.
- Have children say each word and stretch out some words.
- Give sentences to clarify meaning.
- Give specific instructions on how to change words:
  — Add one letter.
  — Change the first letter.
  — Use the same letters.
- Have children clear their holders before making an unrelated word.
- Have children correct their word once it is made in the pocket chart.
- Give children one minute to figure out the secret word and then give them clues.

Sort Words

- Put words in pocket chart in the order made.
- Have children say and spell each word.
- Remind them of how each word was changed to spell the new word.
- Select one word from each rhyming set and line up in columns.
- Let children choose the other words that rhyme.
- Have children pronounce the words.

Transfer Words

- Tell children that they are going to use the rhyming words to spell some new words they might need when they are writing.
- Say the word and a sentence one of your children might write.
- Have children say the word and decide on the beginning letters.
- Write the beginning letters on an index card.
- Take the index card with the beginning letters to the pocket chart and have children say the columns of rhymes and the new word to find the rhyming pattern.
- Write the rhyming pattern on the card to finish the word.
- Have students write the word on paper or a whiteboard.

83

cupcakes

Letters: a e u c c k p s (Patterns **up** and **ue**)

Make: up us use Sue cue cup cap cape cake sake sack pack pace space cupcakes

Sort:

Sue	cake	pace	sack	cup
cue	sake	space	pack	up

Transfer: snack brace track pup due

Make Words

- Have children name and hold up letters.
- Tell children how many letters to use to make each word.
- Have children say each word and stretch out some words.
- Give sentences to clarify meaning.
- Give specific instructions on how to change words:
  — Add one letter.
  — Change the first letter.
  — Use the same letters.
- Have children clear their holders before making an unrelated word.
- Make sure children use a capital **S** when spelling **Sue**.
- Have children correct their word once it is made in the pocket chart.
- Give children one minute to figure out the secret words and then give them clues.

Sort Words

- Put words in pocket chart in the order made.
- Have children say and spell each word.
- Remind them of how each word was changed to spell the new word.
- Select one word from each rhyming set and line up in columns.
- Let children choose the other words that rhyme.
- Have children pronounce the words.

Transfer Words

- Tell children that they are going to use the rhyming words to spell some new words they might need when they are writing.
- Say the word and a sentence one of your children might write.
- Have children say the word and decide on the beginning letters.
- Write the beginning letters on an index card.
- Take the index card with the beginning letters to the pocket chart and have children say the columns of rhymes and the new word to find the rhyming pattern.
- Write the rhyming pattern on the card to finish the word.
- Have students write the word on paper or a whiteboard.

Lesson 59

butterfly

Letters: [e] [u] [b] [f] [l] [r] [t] [t] [y] (Patterns **ue** and **ur**)

Make: fly fry fur bet belt felt left true blue blur blurt
turtle butter flutter butterfly

Sort:

fry	belt	true	butter	fur
fly	felt	blue	flutter	blur
butterfly				

Transfer: melt   sky   clutter   Sue   spur

Make Words

- Have children name and hold up letters.
- Tell children how many letters to use to make each word.
- Have children say each word and stretch out some words.
- Give sentences to clarify meaning.
- Give specific instructions on how to change words:
  — Add one letter.
  — Change the first letter.
  — Use the same letters.
- Have children clear their holders before making an unrelated word.
- Make sure children use a capital **S** when spelling **Sue**.
- Have children correct their word once it is made in the pocket chart.
- Give children one minute to figure out the secret word and then give them clues.

Sort Words

- Put words in pocket chart in the order made.
- Have children say and spell each word.
- Remind them of how each word was changed to spell the new word.
- Select one word from each rhyming set and line up in columns.
- Let children choose the other words that rhyme.
- Have children pronounce the words.

Transfer Words

- Tell children that they are going to use the rhyming words to spell some new words they might need when they are writing.
- Say the word and a sentence one of your children might write.
- Have children say the word and decide on the beginning letters.
- Write the beginning letters on an index card.
- Take the index card with the beginning letters to the pocket chart and have children say the columns of rhymes and the new word to find the rhyming pattern.
- Write the rhyming pattern on the card to finish the word.
- Have students write the word on paper or a whiteboard.

industry

Letters: i u d n r s t y   (Patterns **un**, **une**, **ust**, and **usty**)

Make: try   dry   run   sun   stun   turn   rust   dust   dune   tune
rusty   dusty   study   sturdy   industry

Sort:

run	try	rust	rusty	dune
sun	dry	dust	dusty	tune
stun				

Transfer: just   June   crust   crusty   spy

Make Words

- Have children name and hold up letters.
- Tell children how many letters to use to make each word.
- Have children say each word and stretch out some words.
- Give sentences to clarify meaning.
- Give specific instructions on how to change words:
  — Add one letter.
  — Change the first letter.
  — Use the same letters.
- Have children clear their holders before making an unrelated word.
- Have children correct their word once it is made in the pocket chart.
- Give children one minute to figure out the secret word and then give them clues.

Sort Words

- Put words in pocket chart in the order made.
- Have children say and spell each word.
- Remind them of how each word was changed to spell the new word.
- Select one word from each rhyming set and line up in columns.
- Let children choose the other words that rhyme.
- Have children pronounce the words.

Transfer Words

- Tell children that they are going to use the rhyming words to spell some new words they might need when they are writing.
- Say the word and a sentence one of your children might write.
- Have children say the word and decide on the beginning letters.
- Write the beginning letters on an index card.
- Take the index card with the beginning letters to the pocket chart and have children say the columns of rhymes and the new word to find the rhyming pattern.
- Write the rhyming pattern on the card to finish the word.
- Have students write the word on paper or a whiteboard.

Tell the children to pretend they are writing and need to spell some words. To spell the word, they should stretch out the word and write the beginning letters and then decide which rhyming words will help them finish writing the word. Write these words in columns and have your students chorally pronounce and spell them.

dune	Sue	sun
tune	blue	fun
June	clue	run

Have the children number a sheet of paper from 1 to 5. Say a word and put it in a sentence. Ask your students to stretch out each word to hear the beginning letters and then decide which words it rhymes with to finish spelling the word:

true   spun   prune   glue   stun

Record their responses on your record sheet. If students did not use the correct pattern or beginning letters, record what they did use and analyze their errors.

Word	Beginning Letters	Rhyming Pattern	Word	Beginning Letters	Rhyming Pattern
After Lesson 10			**After Lesson 40**		
drip	dr	ip	plate	pl	ate
yet	y	et	stray	str	ay
chop	ch	op	grain	gr	ain
skip	sk	ip	spray	spr	ay
crop	cr	op	chain	ch	ain
After Lesson 20			**After Lesson 50**		
thick	th	ick	bleed	bl	eed
check	ch	eck	shame	sh	ame
shock	sh	ock	scream	scr	eam
brick	br	ick	greed	gr	eed
clock	cl	ock	stream	str	eam
After Lesson 30			**After Lesson 60**		
flight	fl	ight	true	tr	ue
shine	sh	ine	spun	sp	un
bride	br	ide	prune	pr	une
spine	sp	ine	glue	gl	ue
slight	sl	ight	stun	st	un

Lessons 61-70

These 10 lessons teach the common vowel patterns **oa**, **o-e**, and **or**.

Lesson 61

holidays

Letters: a i o d h l s y (Patterns **old**, **ay**, and **y** as a vowel)

Words to Make: sad had hid lid hay day lay shy sly old
sold hold lady daily holidays

Part One • Making Words

Have the children arrange their letters in front of their holders to match the pocket-chart letters, with the vowel first and the other letters in alphabetical order. Ask the children to hold up and name each letter, noting the capital letter is used to spell names.

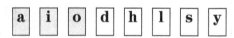

| sad | "The first word we are going to spell is **sad**. I was **sad** when my cat died. Everyone say **sad**. Use 3 letters to spell **sad**." |

Choose a child who has **sad** spelled correctly to spell **sad** with the pocket-chart letters. Have the class chorally spell **sad** and fix their word if **sad** is not correct.

| had | "Change a letter to spell **had**. I **had** strawberry pie for dessert. Everyone say **had**." |

Let a child who has **had** spelled correctly spell **had** with the pocket-chart letters.

| hid | "Change 1 letter to spell **hid**. I **hid** the presents in my closet. Everyone say **hid**." |

Continue the lesson, giving children explicit instruction about which letters to remove and where to add letters. Put each word in a sentence and have children say each word before making it. Have them "stretch" some words to provide practice for children who are still learning to segment words. Let a child who has spelled the word correctly

make that word with the pocket-chart letters. Choose your struggling readers when the word is an easy word and your advanced readers for harder words. Have the children chorally spell each word after it is made in the pocket chart and fix their word to match.

lid	"Change 1 letter to spell **lid**. Put the **lid** on the jar. Everyone say **lid**."
hay	"Use 3 letters to spell **hay**. Horses eat **hay**. Everyone say **hay**."
day	"Change the first letter to spell **day**. We are having a good **day**. Everyone say **day**."
lay	"Change 1 letter to spell **lay**. **Lay** the baby on her stomach. Everyone say **lay**."
shy	"Change 2 letters to spell **shy**. The new student was **shy**. Everyone say **shy**."
sly	"Change a letter to spell **sly**. The detective was clever and **sly**. Everyone say **sly**."
old	"Use 3 letters to spell **old**. How **old** are you? Everyone say **old**."
sold	"Add 1 letter to spell **sold**. Our club **sold** snacks at the game. Everyone say **sold**."
hold	"Change 1 letter to spell **hold**. Can you **hold** the door for me? Everyone say **hold**."
lady	"Use 4 letters to spell **lady**. The **lady** had long red hair. Everyone say **lady**."
daily	"Use 5 letters to spell **daily**. We write a **daily** journal. Everyone say **daily**."
holidays	**(the secret word)** "It's time for the secret word. Signal me if you can figure it out and make it in your holder."

If no one figures out the secret word in one minute, give them a clue.

End the making words part of the lesson by having someone spell **holidays** in the pocket chart and letting everyone hold up their holders to show you **holidays** made in their holders. Have them close the holders and turn their attention to the pocket chart.

Part Two • Sorting Words (Sort for **ad**, **id**, **ay**, **y**, and **old**)

Tell your students that they are going to say all the words they spelled and then sort the rhyming words. Using the index cards with the words, place them in the pocket chart and have the children pronounce them. Remind them of what they changed to make each word.

"First we used 3 letters to spell **sad, s-a-d**."

"We changed a letter to spell **had, h-a-d**."

"We changed the vowel to spell **hid, h-i-d**."

"We changed the first letter to spell **lid, l-i-d**."

"We used 3 letters to spell **day, d-a-y**."

"We changed the first letter to spell **hay, h-a-y**."

"We changed the first letter to spell **lay, l-a-y**."

"We changed two letters to spell **shy, s-h-y**."

"We changed a letter to spell **sly, s-l-y**."

"We used 3 letters to spell **old, o-l-d**."

"We added a letter to spell **sold, s-o-l-d**."

"We changed a letter to spell **hold, h-o-l-d**."

"We used 4 letters to spell **lady, l-a-d-y**."

"We used 5 letters to spell **daily, d-a-i-l-y**."

"We used all our letters to spell the secret word, **holidays, h-o-l-i-d-a-y-s**."

"Now we need to sort out the rhymes. I will take one of each set and you can come and help me find the others."

Arrange one of each set of rhyming words to begin five columns.

had	hid	day	sly	old

Choose five children and help them choose the rhyming words and line them up in columns. Have the rhyming words pronounced and have children notice that they all rhyme and they all have the same letters from the vowel to the end of the word.

had	hid	day	sly	old
sad	lid	hay	shy	hold
		lay		sold

Part Three • Transfer gold bold scold clay

Have the children take out paper. Tell them that you are going to say a word that someone might be writing. By figuring out the rhyming pattern, they will be able to spell the word.

"The first word we are going to spell is **gold**. Rob might be writing that a tale about finding a pot of **gold**. Let's all say **gold** and listen for the beginning letters."

Write **g** on an index card when the children decide that **gold** begins with **g**. Take the index card to the pocket chart and have the children pronounce **gold** with each set of rhyming words. When they decide that **gold** rhymes with **old**, **hold**, and **sold**, write **old** next to **g**. Have children write **gold** on their papers.

Repeat this procedure for **bold**, **scold**, and **clay**.

tractors

Letters: | a | o | c | r | r | s | t | t | (Patterns **oat**, **oats**, and **oast**)

Make: car   tar   cot   rot   trot   cart   star   oats   coats   coast
roast   toast   Oscar   start   tractors

Sort:

oats	cot	star	coast	cart
coats	trot	car	roast	start
	rot	tar	toast	

Transfer: boats   boast   floats   plot

Make Words

- Have children name and hold up letters.
- Tell children how many letters to use to make each word.
- Have children say each word and stretch out some words.
- Give sentences to clarify meaning.
- Give specific instructions on how to change words:
  — Add one letter.
  — Change the first letter.
  — Use the same letters.
- Have children clear their holders before making an unrelated word.
- Make sure children use a capital letter when spelling **Oscar**.
- Have children correct their word once it is made in the pocket chart.
- Give children one minute to figure out the secret word and then give them clues.

Sort Words

- Put words in pocket chart in the order made.
- Have children say and spell each word.
- Remind them of how each word was changed to spell the new word.
- Select one word from each rhyming set and line up in columns.
- Let children choose the other words that rhyme.
- Have children pronounce the words.

Transfer Words

- Tell children that they are going to use the rhyming words to spell some new words they might need when they are writing.
- Say the word and a sentence one of your children might write.
- Have children say the word and decide on the beginning letters.
- Write the beginning letters on an index card.
- Take the index card with the beginning letters to the pocket chart and have children say the columns of rhymes and the new word to find the rhyming pattern.
- Write the rhyming pattern on the card to finish the word.
- Have students write the word on paper or a whiteboard.

Lesson 63

carrots

Letters: `a` `o` `c` `r` `r` `s` `t` (Patterns **ot**, **oast**, **ar**, and **art**)

Make: rat rot cot cat act car art cart star scar coat
coast roast actors carrots

Sort:

cat	cot	art	coast	car
rat	rot	cart	roast	scar
				star

Transfer: toast start chart far

Make Words

- Have children name and hold up letters.
- Tell children how many letters to use to make each word.
- Have children say each word and stretch out some words.
- Give sentences to clarify meaning.
- Give specific instructions on how to change words:
  — Add one letter.
  — Change the first letter.
  — Use the same letters.
- Have children clear their holders before making an unrelated word.
- Have children correct their word once it is made in the pocket chart.
- Give children one minute to figure out the secret word and then give them clues.

Sort Words

- Put words in pocket chart in the order made.
- Have children say and spell each word.
- Remind them of how each word was changed to spell the new word.
- Select one word from each rhyming set and line up in columns.
- Let children choose the other words that rhyme.
- Have children pronounce the words.

Transfer Words

- Tell children that they are going to use the rhyming words to spell some new words they might need when they are writing.
- Say the word and a sentence one of your children might write.
- Have children say the word and decide on the beginning letters.
- Write the beginning letters on an index card.
- Take the index card with the beginning letters to the pocket chart and have children say the columns of rhymes and the new word to find the rhyming pattern.
- Write the rhyming pattern on the card to finish the word.
- Have students write the word on paper or a whiteboard.

Lesson 64

brothers

Letters: | e | o | b | h | r | r | s | t | (Patterns **o**, **ob**, **ose**, and **ore**)

Make: Bo so sob rob robe rose sore more bore tore store shore those throb brothers

Sort:

so	rob	rose	sore
Bo	sob	those	more
	throb		tore
			store
			shore
			bore

Transfer: score   chose   chore   snob

Make Words

- Have children name and hold up letters.
- Tell children how many letters to use to make each word.
- Have children say each word and stretch out some words.
- Give sentences to clarify meaning.
- Give specific instructions on how to change words:
  — Add one letter.
  — Change the first letter.
  — Use the same letters.
- Have children clear their holders before making an unrelated word.
- Make sure children use a capital **B** when spelling **Bo**.
- Have children correct their word once it is made in the pocket chart.
- Give children one minute to figure out the secret word and then give them clues.

Sort Words

- Put words in pocket chart in the order made.
- Have children say and spell each word.
- Remind them of how each word was changed to spell the new word.
- Select one word from each rhyming set and line up in columns.
- Let children choose the other words that rhyme.
- Have children pronounce the words.

Transfer Words

- Tell children that they are going to use the rhyming words to spell some new words they might need when they are writing.
- Say the word and a sentence one of your children might write.
- Have children say the word and decide on the beginning letters.
- Write the beginning letters on an index card.
- Take the index card with the beginning letters to the pocket chart and have children say the columns of rhymes and the new word to find the rhyming pattern.
- Write the rhyming pattern on the card to finish the word.
- Have students write the word on paper or a whiteboard.

raincoats

Letters: | a | a | i | o | c | n | r | s | t | (Patterns **ot**, **oat**, and **oast**)

Make: at sat cat Nat rat rot not cot oat coat rain
cost coast roast raincoats

Sort:

rot	Nat	oat	coast
not	rat	coat	roast
cot	at		
	sat		
	cat		

Transfer: boast   throat   toast   spot

Make Words

- Have children name and hold up letters.
- Tell children how many letters to use to make each word.
- Have children say each word and stretch out some words.
- Give sentences to clarify meaning.
- Give specific instructions on how to change words:
  — Add one letter.
  — Change the first letter.
  — Use the same letters.
- Have children clear their holders before making an unrelated word.
- Make sure children use a capital **N** when spelling **Nat**.
- Have children correct their word once it is made in the pocket chart.
- Give children one minute to figure out the secret word and then give them clues.

Sort Words

- Put words in pocket chart in the order made.
- Have children say and spell each word.
- Remind them of how each word was changed to spell the new word.
- Select one word from each rhyming set and line up in columns.
- Let children choose the other words that rhyme.
- Have children pronounce the words.

Transfer Words

- Tell children that they are going to use the rhyming words to spell some new words they might need when they are writing.
- Say the word and a sentence one of your children might write.
- Have children say the word and decide on the beginning letters.
- Write the beginning letters on an index card.
- Take the index card with the beginning letters to the pocket chart and have children say the columns of rhymes and the new word to find the rhyming pattern.
- Write the rhyming pattern on the card to finish the word.
- Have students write the word on paper or a whiteboard.

Lesson 66

decorates

Letters: | a | e | e | o | c | d | r | s | t | (Patterns **ot**, **ode**, **ore**, **oats**, and **oast**)

Make: cot rot rod rode code core sore tore oats coats
coast roast store decorates

Sort:

coast	rode	cot	sore	oats
roast	code	rot	core	coats
		tore		
		store		

Transfer: shore   score   snore   boats   boast

Make Words

- Have children name and hold up letters.
- Tell children how many letters to use to make each word.
- Have children say each word and stretch out some words.
- Give sentences to clarify meaning.
- Give specific instructions on how to change words:
  — Add one letter.
  — Change the first letter.
  — Use the same letters.
- Have children clear their holders before making an unrelated word.
- Have children correct their word once it is made in the pocket chart.
- Give children one minute to figure out the secret word and then give them clues.

Sort Words

- Put words in pocket chart in the order made.
- Have children say and spell each word.
- Remind them of how each word was changed to spell the new word.
- Select one word from each rhyming set and line up in columns.
- Let children choose the other words that rhyme.
- Have children pronounce the words.

Transfer Words

- Tell children that they are going to use the rhyming words to spell some new words they might need when they are writing.
- Say the word and a sentence one of your children might write.
- Have children say the word and decide on the beginning letters.
- Write the beginning letters on an index card.
- Take the index card with the beginning letters to the pocket chart and have children say the columns of rhymes and the new word to find the rhyming pattern.
- Write the rhyming pattern on the card to finish the word.
- Have students write the word on paper or a whiteboard.

Lesson 67

question

Letters: | e | i | o | u | n | q | s | t | (Pattern **ote**)

Make: sit site nest nose note tone tune quit quiet quite
quote quest question

Sort:

nest	quit	site	note
quest	sit	quite	quote

Transfer: kite   vote   chest   tote   bite

Make Words

- Have children name and hold up letters.
- Tell children how many letters to use to make each word.
- Have children say each word and stretch out some words.
- Give sentences to clarify meaning.
- Give specific instructions on how to change words:
  — Add one letter.
  — Change the first letter.
  — Use the same letters.
- Have children clear their holders before making an unrelated word.
- Have children correct their word once it is made in the pocket chart.
- Give children one minute to figure out the secret word and then give them clues.

Sort Words

- Put words in pocket chart in the order made.
- Have children say and spell each word.
- Remind them of how each word was changed to spell the new word.
- Select one word from each rhyming set and line up in columns.
- Let children choose the other words that rhyme.
- Have children pronounce the words.

Transfer Words

- Tell children that they are going to use the rhyming words to spell some new words they might need when they are writing.
- Say the word and a sentence one of your children might write.
- Have children say the word and decide on the beginning letters.
- Write the beginning letters on an index card.
- Take the index card with the beginning letters to the pocket chart and have children say the columns of rhymes and the new word to find the rhyming pattern.
- Write the rhyming pattern on the card to finish the word.
- Have students write the word on paper or a whiteboard.

Lesson 68

telephones

Letters: `e` `e` `e` `o` `h` `l` `n` `p` `s` `t` (Patterns **ot**, **ose**, **ole**, **ope**, and **one**)

Make: lot   not   note   nose   hose   pose   pole   hole   hope   tone
stone   phone   slope   those   telephones

Sort:

nose	pole	hope	phone	lot
pose	hole	slope	stone	not
hose			tone	

Transfer: clone   throne   scope   chose   those

Make Words

- Have children name and hold up letters.
- Tell children how many letters to use to make each word.
- Have children say each word and stretch out some words.
- Give sentences to clarify meaning.
- Give specific instructions on how to change words:
  — Add one letter.
  — Change the first letter.
  — Use the same letters.
- Have children clear their holders before making an unrelated word.
- Have children correct their word once it is made in the pocket chart.
- Give children one minute to figure out the secret words and then give them clues.

Sort Words

- Put words in pocket chart in the order made.
- Have children say and spell each word.
- Remind them of how each word was changed to spell the new word.
- Select one word from each rhyming set and line up in columns.
- Let children choose the other words that rhyme.
- Have children pronounce the words.

Transfer Words

- Tell children that they are going to use the rhyming words to spell some new words they might need when they are writing.
- Say the word and a sentence one of your children might write.
- Have children say the word and decide on the beginning letters.
- Write the beginning letters on an index card.
- Take the index card with the beginning letters to the pocket chart and have children say the columns of rhymes and the new word to find the rhyming pattern.
- Write the rhyming pattern on the card to finish the word.
- Have students write the word on paper or a whiteboard.

Lesson 69

reporters

Letters: | e | e | o | p | r | r | r | s | t | (Patterns **op**, **ot**, **ort**, and **ore**)

Make: see top pot spot stop sort port tree sore tore
store sport report reporters

Sort:

top	pot	sort	see	sore
stop	spot	port	spree	tore
		sport	tree	

Transfer: short shore chore chop jot

Make Words

- Have children name and hold up letters.
- Tell children how many letters to use to make each word.
- Have children say each word and stretch out some words.
- Give sentences to clarify meaning.
- Give specific instructions on how to change words:
  — Add one letter.
  — Change the first letter.
  — Use the same letters.
- Have children clear their holders before making an unrelated word.
- Have children correct their word once it is made in the pocket chart.
- Give children one minute to figure out the secret word and then give them clues.

Sort Words

- Put words in pocket chart in the order made.
- Have children say and spell each word.
- Remind them of how each word was changed to spell the new word.
- Select one word from each rhyming set and line up in columns.
- Let children choose the other words that rhyme.
- Have children pronounce the words.

Transfer Words

- Tell children that they are going to use the rhyming words to spell some new words they might need when they are writing.
- Say the word and a sentence one of your children might write.
- Have children say the word and decide on the beginning letters.
- Write the beginning letters on an index card.
- Take the index card with the beginning letters to the pocket chart and have children say the columns of rhymes and the new word to find the rhyming pattern.
- Write the rhyming pattern on the card to finish the word.
- Have students write the word on paper or a whiteboard.

tornado

Letters: a o o d n r t (Patterns **od** and **oat**)

Make: art and ant Nat rat rot not nod rod road toad
dart torn tornado

Sort:

art	rat	rot	rod	toad
dart	Nate	not	nod	road

Transfer: start load prod trot shot

Make Words

- Have children name and hold up letters.
- Tell children how many letters to use to make each word.
- Have children say each word and stretch out some words.
- Give sentences to clarify meaning.
- Give specific instructions on how to change words:
  — Add one letter.
  — Change the first letter.
  — Use the same letters.
- Have children clear their holders before making an unrelated word.
- Make sure children use a capital **N** when spelling **Nate**.
- Have children correct their word once it is made in the pocket chart.
- Give children one minute to figure out the secret word and then give them clues.

Sort Words

- Put words in pocket chart in the order made.
- Have children say and spell each word.
- Remind them of how each word was changed to spell the new word.
- Select one word from each rhyming set and line up in columns.
- Let children choose the other words that rhyme.
- Have children pronounce the words.

Transfer Words

- Tell children that they are going to use the rhyming words to spell some new words they might need when they are writing.
- Say the word and a sentence one of your children might write.
- Have children say the word and decide on the beginning letters.
- Write the beginning letters on an index card.
- Take the index card with the beginning letters to the pocket chart and have children say the columns of rhymes and the new word to find the rhyming pattern.
- Write the rhyming pattern on the card to finish the word.
- Have students write the word on paper or a whiteboard.

Assessment Lessons 61-70

Tell the children to pretend they are writing and need to spell some words. To spell the word, they should stretch out the word and write the beginning letters and then decide which rhyming words will help them finish writing the word. Write these words in columns and have your students chorally pronounce and spell them.

more	port	art
sore	sort	part
store	sport	cart

Have the children number a sheet of paper from 1 to 5. Say a word and put it in a sentence. Ask your students to stretch out each word to hear the beginning letters and then decide which words it rhymes with to finish spelling the word:

smart   score   short   chore   snore

Record their responses on your record sheet. If students did not use the correct pattern or beginning letters, record what they did use and analyze their errors.

Word	Beginning Letters	Rhyming Pattern
After Lesson 10		
drip	dr	ip
yet	y	et
chop	ch	op
skip	sk	ip
crop	cr	op
After Lesson 20		
thick	th	ick
check	ch	eck
shock	sh	ock
brick	br	ick
clock	cl	ock
After Lesson 30		
flight	fl	ight
shine	sh	ine
bride	br	ide
spine	sp	ine
slight	sl	ight

Word	Beginning Letters	Rhyming Pattern
After Lesson 40		
plate	pl	ate
stray	str	ay
grain	gr	ain
spray	spr	ay
chain	ch	ain
After Lesson 50		
bleed	bl	eed
shame	sh	ame
scream	scr	eam
greed	gr	eed
stream	str	eam
After Lesson 60		
true	tr	ue
spun	sp	un
prune	pr	une
glue	gl	ue
stun	st	un
After Lesson 70		
smart	sm	art
short	sh	ort
score	sc	ore
chore	ch	ore
snore	sn	ore

Lessons 71-80

These 10 lessons teach the common vowel patterns **oo**, **oy**, **oi**, and **ou**.

Lesson 71

cartoons

Letters: a o o c n r s t (Patterns **on**, **ot**, **oast**, **orn**, and **oon**)

Words to Make: on Ron not cot soon torn corn coat coast
roast roost acorn actors cartons cartoons

Part One • Making Words

Have the children arrange their letters in front of their holders to match the pocket-chart letters, with the vowel first and the other letters in alphabetical order. Ask the children to hold up and name each letter, noting the capital letter is used to spell names.

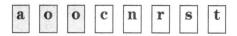

on — "The first word we are going to spell is **on**. My can was sleeping **on** my bed. Everyone say **on**. Use 2 letters to spell **on**."

Choose a child who has **on** spelled correctly to spell **on** with the pocket-chart letters. Have the class chorally spell **on** and fix their word if **on** is not correct.

Ron — "Add a letter to spell **Ron**. Do you know anyone named **Ron**? Everyone say **Ron**."

Let a child who has **Ron** spelled correctly spell **Ron** with the pocket-chart letters.

not — "Use 3 letters to spell **not**. It is **not** a rainy day. Everyone say **not**."

Continue the lesson, giving children explicit instruction about which letters to remove and where to add letters. Put each word in a sentence and have children say each word before making it. Have them "stretch" some words to provide practice for children who are still learning to segment words. Let a child who has spelled the word correctly make that word with the pocket-chart letters. Choose your struggling readers when the word is an easy word and your advanced readers for harder words. Have the children chorally spell each word after it is made in the pocket chart and fix their word to match.

cot	"Change 1 letter to spell **cot**. Did you ever sleep on a **cot**? Everyone say **cot**."
soon	"Use 4 letters to spell **soon**. We will go to lunch **soon**. Everyone say **soon**."
torn	"Use 4 letters to spell **torn**. This paper is **torn**. Everyone say **torn**."
corn	"Use 4 letters to spell **corn**. Do you like **corn** on the cob? Everyone say **corn**."
coat	"Change 2 letters to spell **coat**. I have a new red **coat**. Everyone say **coat**."
coast	"Add a letter to spell **coast**. Do you **coast** down the hill on your bike? Everyone say **coast**."
roast	"Change 1 letter to spell **roast**. Did you ever **roast** marshmallows? Everyone say **roast**."
roost	"Change 1 letter to spell **roost**. At night, the birds **roost** in the trees. Everyone say **roost**."
acorn	"Use 5 letters to spell **acorn**. The squirrel was eating an **acorn**. Everyone say **acorn**."
actors	"Use 6 letters to spell **actors**. People who act in plays are called **actors**. Everyone say **actors**."
cartons	"Use 7 letters to spell **cartons**. At lunch, our milk comes in **cartons**. Everyone say **cartons**."
cartoons	**(the secret word)** "It's time for the secret word. Signal me if you can figure it out and make it in your holder."

If no one figures out the secret word in one minute, give them a clue.

End the making words part of the lesson by having someone spell **cartoons** in the pocket chart and letting everyone hold up their holders to show you **cartoons** made in their holders. Have them close the holders and turn their attention to the pocket chart.

Part Two • Sorting Words (Sort for **on**, **not**, **orn**, and **oast**)

Using the index cards with the words, place them in the pocket chart and have the children pronounce them. Remind them of what they changed to make each word.

"First we used 2 letters to spell **on**, o-n."

"We added a letter to spell **Ron**, R-o-n."

"We used 3 letters to spell **not**, n-o-t."

"We changed the first letter to spell **cot**, c-o-t."

"We used 4 letters to spell **soon**, s-o-o-n."

"We used 4 letters to spell **torn**, t-o-r-n."

"We changed the first letter to spell **corn, c-o-r-n**."

"We changed the last 2 letters to spell **coat, c-o-a-t**."

"We added the s to spell **coast, c-o-a-s-t**."

"We changed the first letter to spell **roast, r-o-a-s-t**."

"We changed 1 letter to spell **roost, r-o-o-s-t**."

"We used 5 letters to spell **acorn, a-c-o-r-n**."

"We used 6 letters to spell **actors, a-c-t-o-r-s**."

"We used 7 letters to spell **cartons, c-a-r-t-o-n-s**."

"We used all our letters to spell the secret word, **cartoons, c-a-r-t-o-o-n-s**."

"Now we need to sort out the rhymes. I will take one of each set and you can come and help me find the others."

Arrange one of each set of rhyming words to begin columns.

on	corn	coast	not

Choose four children to find the other rhyming words.

on	corn	coast	not
Ron	torn	roast	cot

Part Three ● Transfer born toast horn pot plot

Have the children take out paper. Tell them that you are going to say a word that someone might be writing. By figuring out the rhyming pattern, they will be able to spell the word.

"The first word we are going to spell is **born**. Carlton might be writing that he was **born** on Saturday. Let's all say **born** and listen for the beginning letters."

Write **b** on an index card. Take the index card to the pocket chart and have the children pronounce **born** with each set of rhyming words. When they decide that **born** rhymes with **corn** and **torn**, write **orn** next to **b**. Have children write **born** on their papers.

Repeat this procedure for **toast**, **horn**, **pot**, and **plot**.

shortstop

Letters: o o h p r s s t t (Patterns **op**, **ot**, **oot**, and **oops**)

Make: hot shot root hoot stop shop hops hoops tooth
shoot short stoop stoops troops shortstop

Sort:

root	stop	shot	stoops
hoot	shop	hot	troops
	shortstop		hoops

Transfer: scoops   boot   swoops   plop   pot

Make Words

- Have children name and hold up letters.
- Tell children how many letters to use to make each word.
- Have children say each word and stretch out some words.
- Give sentences to clarify meaning.
- Give specific instructions on how to change words:
  — Add one letter.
  — Change the first letter.
  — Use the same letters.
- Have children clear their holders before making an unrelated word.
- Have children correct their word once it is made in the pocket chart.
- Give children one minute to figure out the secret word and then give them clues.

Sort Words

- Put words in pocket chart in the order made.
- Have children say and spell each word.
- Remind them of how each word was changed to spell the new word.
- Select one word from each rhyming set and line up in columns.
- Let children choose the other words that rhyme.
- Have children pronounce the words.

Transfer Words

- Tell children that they are going to use the rhyming words to spell some new words they might need when they are writing.
- Say the word and a sentence one of your children might write.
- Have children say the word and decide on the beginning letters.
- Write the beginning letters on an index card.
- Take the index card with the beginning letters to the pocket chart and have children say the columns of rhymes and the new word to find the rhyming pattern.
- Write the rhyming pattern on the card to finish the word.
- Have students write the word on paper or a whiteboard.

Lesson 73

chocolate

Letters: | a | e | o | o | c | c | h | l | t | (Patterns **ool** and **oot**)

Make: eat ate late hate heat each cool tool hoot loot
teach cheat coach chocolate

Sort:

heat	cool	loot	each	ate
cheat	tool	hoot	teach	late
eat				hate

Transfer: pool fool scoot plate root

Make Words

- Have children name and hold up letters.
- Tell children how many letters to use to make each word.
- Have children say each word and stretch out some words.
- Give sentences to clarify meaning.
- Give specific instructions on how to change words:
  — Add one letter.
  — Change the first letter.
  — Use the same letters.
- Have children clear their holders before making an unrelated word.
- Have children correct their word once it is made in the pocket chart.
- Give children one minute to figure out the secret word and then give them clues.

Sort Words

- Put words in pocket chart in the order made.
- Have children say and spell each word.
- Remind them of how each word was changed to spell the new word.
- Select one word from each rhyming set and line up in columns.
- Let children choose the other words that rhyme.
- Have children pronounce the words.

Transfer Words

- Tell children that they are going to use the rhyming words to spell some new words they might need when they are writing.
- Say the word and a sentence one of your children might write.
- Have children say the word and decide on the beginning letters.
- Write the beginning letters on an index card.
- Take the index card with the beginning letters to the pocket chart and have children say the columns of rhymes and the new word to find the rhyming pattern.
- Write the rhyming pattern on the card to finish the word.
- Have students write the word on paper or a whiteboard.

bedrooms

Letters: e o o b d m r s (Patterns **oom** and **ore**)

Make:	Ed bed sob rob robe bore more sore rose		
	room boom broom bedrooms		

Sort:	Ed	more	rob	room
	bed	sore	sob	boon
		bore		broom

Transfer:	zoom	bloom	groom	tore	shed

Make Words

- Have children name and hold up letters.
- Tell children how many letters to use to make each word.
- Have children say each word and stretch out some words.
- Give sentences to clarify meaning.
- Give specific instructions on how to change words:
    — Add one letter.
    — Change the first letter.
    — Use the same letters.
- Have children clear their holders before making an unrelated word.
- Make sure children use a capital **E** when spelling **Ed**.
- Have children correct their word once it is made in the pocket chart.
- Give children one minute to figure out the secret word and then give them clues.

Sort Words

- Put words in pocket chart in the order made.
- Have children say and spell each word.
- Remind them of how each word was changed to spell the new word.
- Select one word from each rhyming set and line up in columns.
- Let children choose the other words that rhyme.
- Have children pronounce the words.

Transfer Words

- Tell children that they are going to use the rhyming words to spell some new words they might need when they are writing.
- Say the word and a sentence one of your children might write.
- Have children say the word and decide on the beginning letters.
- Write the beginning letters on an index card.
- Take the index card with the beginning letters to the pocket chart and have children say the columns of rhymes and the new word to find the rhyming pattern.
- Write the rhyming pattern on the card to finish the word.
- Have students write the word on paper or a whiteboard.

Lesson 75

notebooks

Letters: | e | o | o | o | b | k | n | s | t | (Patterns **ook** and **one**)

Make: ten   Ben   Ken   set   bet   net   not   note   tone   took   book
stone   boots   notebooks

Sort:

Ben	bet	took	tone
Ken	set	book	stone
ten	net		

Transfer: shook   brook   phone   then   bone

Make Words

- Have children name and hold up letters.
- Tell children how many letters to use to make each word.
- Have children say each word and stretch out some words.
- Give sentences to clarify meaning.
- Give specific instructions on how to change words:
  — Add one letter.
  — Change the first letter.
  — Use the same letters.
- Have children clear their holders before making an unrelated word.
- Make sure children use capital letters when spelling names.
- Have children correct their word once it is made in the pocket chart.
- Give children one minute to figure out the secret word and then give them clues.

Sort Words

- Put words in pocket chart in the order made.
- Have children say and spell each word.
- Remind them of how each word was changed to spell the new word.
- Select one word from each rhyming set and line up in columns.
- Let children choose the other words that rhyme.
- Have children pronounce the words.

Transfer Words

- Tell children that they are going to use the rhyming words to spell some new words they might need when they are writing.
- Say the word and a sentence one of your children might write.
- Have children say the word and decide on the beginning letters.
- Write the beginning letters on an index card.
- Take the index card with the beginning letters to the pocket chart and have children say the columns of rhymes and the new word to find the rhyming pattern.
- Write the rhyming pattern on the card to finish the word.
- Have students write the word on paper or a whiteboard.

Lesson 76

factory

Letters: a o c f r t y (Patterns **oy** and **or**)

Make: or for far car act fry try toy Roy Ray tray fact
fort forty factory

Sort:

far	fry	or	toy	Ray	act
car	try	for	Roy	tray	fact

Transfer: joy spray stray cry

Make Words

- Have children name and hold up letters.
- Tell children how many letters to use to make each word.
- Have children say each word and stretch out some words.
- Give sentences to clarify meaning.
- Give specific instructions on how to change words:
  — Add one letter.
  — Change the first letter.
  — Use the same letters.
- Have children clear their holders before making an unrelated word.
- Make sure children use capital letters when spelling names.
- Have children correct their word once it is made in the pocket chart.
- Give children one minute to figure out the secret word and then give them clues.

Sort Words

- Put words in pocket chart in the order made.
- Have children say and spell each word.
- Remind them of how each word was changed to spell the new word.
- Select one word from each rhyming set and line up in columns.
- Let children choose the other words that rhyme.
- Have children pronounce the words.

Transfer Words

- Tell children that they are going to use the rhyming words to spell some new words they might need when they are writing.
- Say the word and a sentence one of your children might write.
- Have children say the word and decide on the beginning letters.
- Write the beginning letters on an index card.
- Take the index card with the beginning letters to the pocket chart and have children say the columns of rhymes and the new word to find the rhyming pattern.
- Write the rhyming pattern on the card to finish the word.
- Have students write the word on paper or a whiteboard.

Lesson 77
history

Letters: | i | o | h | r | s | t | y | (Patterns **ort**, **oy**, and **y** as a vowel)

Make: is his shy try toy Roy sir stir sort short shirt story history

Sort:

shy	Roy	sir	is	short
try	toy	stir	his	sort

Transfer: sport   fort   Troy   port

Make Words

- Have children name and hold up letters.
- Tell children how many letters to use to make each word.
- Have children say each word and stretch out some words.
- Give sentences to clarify meaning.
- Give specific instructions on how to change words:
  — Add one letter.
  — Change the first letter.
  — Use the same letters.
- Have children clear their holders before making an unrelated word.
- Make sure children use capital letters when spelling names.
- Have children correct their word once it is made in the pocket chart.
- Give children one minute to figure out the secret word and then give them clues.

Sort Words

- Put words in pocket chart in the order made.
- Have children say and spell each word.
- Remind them of how each word was changed to spell the new word.
- Select one word from each rhyming set and line up in columns.
- Let children choose the other words that rhyme.
- Have children pronounce the words.

Transfer Words

- Tell children that they are going to use the rhyming words to spell some new words they might need when they are writing.
- Say the word and a sentence one of your children might write.
- Have children say the word and decide on the beginning letters.
- Write the beginning letters on an index card.
- Take the index card with the beginning letters to the pocket chart and have children say the columns of rhymes and the new word to find the rhyming pattern.
- Write the rhyming pattern on the card to finish the word.
- Have students write the word on paper or a whiteboard.

Lesson 78

sailboats

Letters: | a | a | i | o | b | l | s | s | t | (Patterns **oil** and **ail**)

Make: Al Sal sat bat oil boil soil sail tail bail bait last blast boats sailboats

Sort:

oil	Al	bat	sail	last
boil	Sal	sat	bail	blast
soil			tail	

Transfer: broil trail spoil snail

Make Words

- Have children name and hold up letters.
- Tell children how many letters to use to make each word.
- Have children say each word and stretch out some words.
- Give sentences to clarify meaning.
- Give specific instructions on how to change words:
  — Add one letter.
  — Change the first letter.
  — Use the same letters.
- Have children clear their holders before making an unrelated word.
- Make sure children use capital letters when spelling names.
- Have children correct their word once it is made in the pocket chart.
- Give children one minute to figure out the secret words and then give them clues.

Sort Words

- Put words in pocket chart in the order made.
- Have children say and spell each word.
- Remind them of how each word was changed to spell the new word.
- Select one word from each rhyming set and line up in columns.
- Let children choose the other words that rhyme.
- Have children pronounce the words.

Transfer Words

- Tell children that they are going to use the rhyming words to spell some new words they might need when they are writing.
- Say the word and a sentence one of your children might write.
- Have children say the word and decide on the beginning letters.
- Write the beginning letters on an index card.
- Take the index card with the beginning letters to the pocket chart and have children say the columns of rhymes and the new word to find the rhyming pattern.
- Write the rhyming pattern on the card to finish the word.
- Have students write the word on paper or a whiteboard.

Lesson 79

playground

Letters: a o u d g l n r p y (Patterns **oud** and **ound**)

Make: pay play pony road load loud aloud along proud
pound round ground around dragon playground

Sort:

play	loud	pound
pay	proud	round
		ground
		playground

Transfer: cloud sound found tray

Make Words

- Have children name and hold up letters.
- Tell children how many letters to use to make each word.
- Have children say each word and stretch out some words.
- Give sentences to clarify meaning.
- Give specific instructions on how to change words:
  — Add one letter.
  — Change the first letter.
  — Use the same letters.
- Have children clear their holders before making an unrelated word.
- Have children correct their word once it is made in the pocket chart.
- Give children one minute to figure out the secret word and then give them clues.

Sort Words

- Put words in pocket chart in the order made.
- Have children say and spell each word.
- Remind them of how each word was changed to spell the new word.
- Select one word from each rhyming set and line up in columns.
- Let children choose the other words that rhyme.
- Have children pronounce the words.

Transfer Words

- Tell children that they are going to use the rhyming words to spell some new words they might need when they are writing.
- Say the word and a sentence one of your children might write.
- Have children say the word and decide on the beginning letters.
- Write the beginning letters on an index card.
- Take the index card with the beginning letters to the pocket chart and have children say the columns of rhymes and the new word to find the rhyming pattern.
- Write the rhyming pattern on the card to finish the word.
- Have students write the word on paper or a whiteboard.

Lesson 80

shouting

Letters: | i | o | u | g | h | n | s | t | (Patterns **ot**, **ut**, and **out**)

Make: out   hut   hit   hot   not   nut   shut   shot   thin   thing
night   sight   south   shout   shouting

Sort:

out	sight	nut	shot
shout	night	shut	not
			hot

Transfer: scout   trout   pout   flight

Make Words

- Have children name and hold up letters.
- Tell children how many letters to use to make each word.
- Have children say each word and stretch out some words.
- Give sentences to clarify meaning.
- Give specific instructions on how to change words:
  — Add one letter.
  — Change the first letter.
  — Use the same letters.
- Have children clear their holders before making an unrelated word.
- Have children correct their word once it is made in the pocket chart.
- Give children one minute to figure out the secret word and then give them clues.

Sort Words

- Put words in pocket chart in the order made.
- Have children say and spell each word.
- Remind them of how each word was changed to spell the new word.
- Select one word from each rhyming set and line up in columns.
- Let children choose the other words that rhyme.
- Have children pronounce the words.

Transfer Words

- Tell children that they are going to use the rhyming words to spell some new words they might need when they are writing.
- Say the word and a sentence one of your children might write.
- Have children say the word and decide on the beginning letters.
- Write the beginning letters on an index card.
- Take the index card with the beginning letters to the pocket chart and have children say the columns of rhymes and the new word to find the rhyming pattern.
- Write the rhyming pattern on the card to finish the word.
- Have students write the word on paper or a whiteboard.

Tell the children to pretend they are writing and need to spell some words. To spell the word, they should stretch out the word and write the beginning letters and then decide which rhyming words will help them finish writing the word. Write these words in columns and have your students chorally pronounce and spell them.

cool	oil	sail
pool	boil	tail
school	soil	pail

Have the children number a sheet of paper from 1 to 5. Say a word and put it in a sentence. Ask your students to stretch out each word to hear the beginning letters and then decide which words it rhymes with to finish spelling the word:

spoil   snail   stool   broil   drool

Record their responses on your record sheet. If students did not use the correct pattern or beginning letters, record what they did use and analyze their errors.

Word	Beginning Letters	Rhyming Pattern
After Lesson 10		
drip	dr	ip
yet	y	et
chop	ch	op
skip	sk	ip
crop	cr	op
After Lesson 20		
thick	th	ick
check	ch	eck
shock	sh	ock
brick	br	ick
clock	cl	ock
After Lesson 30		
flight	fl	ight
shine	sh	ine
bride	br	ide
spine	sp	ine
slight	sl	ight

Word	Beginning Letters	Rhyming Pattern
After Lesson 40		
plate	pl	ate
stray	str	ay
grain	gr	ain
spray	spr	ay
chain	ch	ain
After Lesson 50		
bleed	bl	eed
shame	sh	ame
scream	scr	eam
greed	gr	eed
stream	str	eam
After Lesson 60		
true	tr	ue
spun	sp	un
prune	pr	une
glue	gl	ue
stun	st	un
After Lesson 70		
smart	sm	art
short	sh	ort
score	sc	ore
chore	ch	ore
snore	sn	ore
After Lesson 80		
spool	sp	ool
snail	sn	ail
stool	st	ool
broil	br	oil
drool	dr	ool

Lessons 81-90

These 10 lessons teach the common vowel patterns **all**, **ell**, **ill**, **ow**, and **aw**.

Lesson 81

lollipops

Letters: i   o   o   l   l   l   p   p   s   (Patterns **op**, **oil**, **oop**, and **ool**)

Words to Make: pop,   lip,   oil,   soil,   silo,   plop,   pool,   loop,   polo,
slip,   pill,   spill,   spoil,   spool,   lollipops

Part One • Making Words

Have the children arrange their letters in front of their holders to match the pocket-chart letters, with the vowel first and the other letters in alphabetical order. Ask the children to hold up and name each letter, noting the capital letter is used to spell names.

pop   "The first word we are going to spell is **pop**. Did you **pop** the balloon? Everyone say **pop**. Use 3 letters to spell **pop**."

Choose a child who has **pop** spelled correctly to spell **pop** with the pocket-chart letters. Have the class chorally spell **pop** and fix their word if **pop** is not correct.

lip   "Use 3 letters to spell **lip**. The baby fell and cut her **lip**. Everyone say **lip**."

Let a child who has **lip** spelled correctly spell **lip** with the pocket-chart letters.

oil   "Use 3 letters to spell **oil**. I took my car in for an **oil** change. Everyone say **oil**."

Continue the lesson, giving children explicit instruction about which letters to remove and where to add letters. Put each word in a sentence and have children say each word before making it. Have them "stretch" some words to provide practice for children who are still learning to segment words. Let a child who has spelled the word correctly

make that word with the pocket-chart letters. Choose your struggling readers when the word is an easy word and your advanced readers for harder words. Have the children chorally spell each word after it is made in the pocket chart and fix their word to match.

soil	"Add 1 letter to spell **soil**. We planted the seeds in rich **soil**. Everyone say **soil**."
silo	"Use the same letters to spell **silo**. Corn is stored in a **silo**. Everyone say **silo**."
plop	"Use 4 letters to spell **plop**. When I am tired, I **plop** on the sofa and take a nap. Everyone say **plop**."
pool	"Use 4 letters to spell **pool**. I like to swim in the **pool**. Everyone say **pool**."
loop	"Use the same letters to spell **loop**. You make a **loop** when you tie your shoes. Everyone say **loop**."
polo	"Use the same letters again to spell **polo**. I think it would be fun to play **polo**. Everyone say **polo**."
slip	"Use 4 letters to spell **slip**. Did you ever **slip** and fall on the ice? Everyone say **slip**."
pill	"Use 4 letters to spell **pill**. I take a vitamin **pill** every day. Everyone say **pill**."
spill	"Add 1 letter to spell **spill**. Did you ever **spill** your milk? Everyone say **spill**."
spoil	"Use 5 letters to spell **spoil**. Don't **spoil** the surprise by telling your brother about the party. Everyone say **spoil**."
spool	"Change 1 letter to spell **spool**. I need a **spool** of blue thread. Everyone say **spool**."
lollipops	**(the secret word)** "It's time for the secret word. Signal me if you can figure it out and make it in your holder."

If no one figures out the secret word in one minute, give them a clue.

End the making words part of the lesson by having someone spell **lollipops** in the pocket chart and letting everyone hold up their holders to show you **lollipops** made in their holders. Have them close the holders and turn their attention to the pocket chart.

Part Two • Sorting Words (Sort for **op**, **ip**, **oil**, **oop**, and **ool**)

Using the index cards with the words, place them in the pocket chart and have the children pronounce them. Remind them of what they changed to make each word.

"First we used 3 letters to spell **pop**, **p-o-p**."

"We used 3 letters to spell **lip**, **l-i-p**."

"We used 3 letters to spell **oil**, **o-i-l**."

"We added a letter to spell **soil**, **s-o-i-l**."

"We moved the letters to spell **silo**, **s-i-l-o**."

"We used 4 letters to spell **plop, p-l-o-p**."

"We used 4 letters to spell **pool, p-o-o-l**."

"We moved the letters to spell **loop, l-o-o-p**."

"We used the same letters again to spell **polo, p-o-l-o**."

"We used 4 letters to spell **slip, s-l-i-p**."

"We used 4 letters to spell **pill, p-i-l-l**."

"We added a letter to spell **spill, s-p-i-l-l**."

"We used 5 letters to spell **spoil, s-p-o-i-l**."

"We changed 1 letter to spell **spool, s-p-o-o-l**."

"We used all our letters to spell the secret word, **lollipops, l-o-l-l-i-p-o-p-s**."

"Now we need to sort out the rhymes. I will take one of each set and you can come and help me find the others."

Arrange one of each set of rhyming words to begin five columns.

pop	**lip**	**oil**	**loop**	**pool**

Choose five children to find the other rhyming words.

pop	**lip**	**oil**	**pill**	**pool**
plop	**slip**	**spoil**	**spill**	**spool**
		soil		

Part Three • Transfer   thrill drill chill foil cool

Have the children take out paper. Tell them that you are going to say a word that someone might be writing. By figuring out the rhyming pattern, they will be able to spell the word.

"The first word we are going to spell is **thrill**. Jen might be writing that riding the roller coaster was a **thrill**. Let's all say **thrill** and listen for the beginning letters."

Write **thr** on an index card. Take the index card to the pocket chart and have the children pronounce **thrill** with each set of rhyming words. When they decide that **thrill** rhymes with **pill** and **spill**, write **ill** next to **thr**. Have children write **thrill** on their papers.

Repeat this procedure for **drill, chill, foil,** and **cool**.

football

Letters: `a` `o` `o` `b` `f` `l` `l` `t` (Patterns **ool**, **oat**, and **all**)

Make: at bat fat all ball fall tall flat tool fool foot
boat float ballot football

Sort:

tool	float	all	bat
fool	boat	fall	at
		tall	fat
		ball	flat
		football	

Transfer: mall stool stall coat

Make Words

- Have children name and hold up letters.
- Tell children how many letters to use to make each word.
- Have children say each word and stretch out some words.
- Give sentences to clarify meaning.
- Give specific instructions on how to change words:
  — Add one letter.
  — Change the first letter.
  — Use the same letters.
- Have children clear their holders before making an unrelated word.
- Have children correct their word once it is made in the pocket chart.
- Give children one minute to figure out the secret word and then give them clues.

Sort Words

- Put words in pocket chart in the order made.
- Have children say and spell each word.
- Remind them of how each word was changed to spell the new word.
- Select one word from each rhyming set and line up in columns.
- Let children choose the other words that rhyme.
- Have children pronounce the words.

Transfer Words

- Tell children that they are going to use the rhyming words to spell some new words they might need when they are writing.
- Say the word and a sentence one of your children might write.
- Have children say the word and decide on the beginning letters.
- Write the beginning letters on an index card.
- Take the index card with the beginning letters to the pocket chart and have children say the columns of rhymes and the new word to find the rhyming pattern.
- Write the rhyming pattern on the card to finish the word.
- Have students write the word on paper or a whiteboard.

Lesson 83

smaller

Letters: a e l l m r s (Patterns **all** and **ell**)

Make: at Al all mall male sale seal real meal lame same
sell smell small smaller

Sort:

all	smell	sale	lame	real
small	sell	male	same	meal
mall				seal

Transfer: swell   yell   flame   cane

Make Words

- Have children name and hold up letters.
- Tell children how many letters to use to make each word.
- Have children say each word and stretch out some words.
- Give sentences to clarify meaning.
- Give specific instructions on how to change words:
  — Add one letter.
  — Change the first letter.
  — Use the same letters.
- Have children clear their holders before making an unrelated word.
- Have children correct their word once it is made in the pocket chart.
- Give children one minute to figure out the secret word and then give them clues.

Sort Words

- Put words in pocket chart in the order made.
- Have children say and spell each word.
- Remind them of how each word was changed to spell the new word.
- Select one word from each rhyming set and line up in columns.
- Let children choose the other words that rhyme.
- Have children pronounce the words.

Transfer Words

- Tell children that they are going to use the rhyming words to spell some new words they might need when they are writing.
- Say the word and a sentence one of your children might write.
- Have children say the word and decide on the beginning letters.
- Write the beginning letters on an index card.
- Take the index card with the beginning letters to the pocket chart and have children say the columns of rhymes and the new word to find the rhyming pattern.
- Write the rhyming pattern on the card to finish the word.
- Have students write the word on paper or a whiteboard.

Lesson 84

waterfall

Letters: | a | a | e | f | l | l | r | t | w | (Patterns **all** and **ell**)

Make: at ate all rat rate late raft tell well fell fall
wall tall taller waterfall

Sort:

at	fall	rate	well
rat	tall	late	fell
	wall	ate	tell
	all		
	waterfall		

Transfer: small   smell   shell   slate

Make Words

- Have children name and hold up letters.
- Tell children how many letters to use to make each word.
- Have children say each word and stretch out some words.
- Give sentences to clarify meaning.
- Give specific instructions on how to change words:
  — Add one letter.
  — Change the first letter.
  — Use the same letters.
- Have children clear their holders before making an unrelated word.
- Have children correct their word once it is made in the pocket chart.
- Give children one minute to figure out the secret word and then give them clues.

Sort Words

- Put words in pocket chart in the order made.
- Have children say and spell each word.
- Remind them of how each word was changed to spell the new word.
- Select one word from each rhyming set and line up in columns.
- Let children choose the other words that rhyme.
- Have children pronounce the words.

Transfer Words

- Tell children that they are going to use the rhyming words to spell some new words they might need when they are writing.
- Say the word and a sentence one of your children might write.
- Have children say the word and decide on the beginning letters.
- Write the beginning letters on an index card.
- Take the index card with the beginning letters to the pocket chart and have children say the columns of rhymes and the new word to find the rhyming pattern.
- Write the rhyming pattern on the card to finish the word.
- Have students write the word on paper or a whiteboard.

Lesson 85

volleyball

Letters: | a | e | o | b | l | l | l | l | v | y | (Patterns **all** and **ell**)

Make: boy bay lay all ball bell yell able love above valley
volley lovely lovable volleyball

Sort:

bell	all	bay	love
yell	ball	lay	above

Transfer: stall shove dwell wall smell

Make Words

- Have children name and hold up letters.
- Tell children how many letters to use to make each word.
- Have children say each word and stretch out some words.
- Give sentences to clarify meaning.
- Give specific instructions on how to change words:
  — Add one letter.
  — Change the first letter.
  — Use the same letters.
- Have children clear their holders before making an unrelated word.
- Have children correct their word once it is made in the pocket chart.
- Give children one minute to figure out the secret word and then give them clues.

Sort Words

- Put words in pocket chart in the order made.
- Have children say and spell each word.
- Remind them of how each word was changed to spell the new word.
- Select one word from each rhyming set and line up in columns.
- Let children choose the other words that rhyme.
- Have children pronounce the words.

Transfer Words

- Tell children that they are going to use the rhyming words to spell some new words they might need when they are writing.
- Say the word and a sentence one of your children might write.
- Have children say the word and decide on the beginning letters.
- Write the beginning letters on an index card.
- Take the index card with the beginning letters to the pocket chart and have children say the columns of rhymes and the new word to find the rhyming pattern.
- Write the rhyming pattern on the card to finish the word.
- Have students write the word on paper or a whiteboard.

slowpoke

Letters: e o o k l p s w   (Patterns two sounds for **ow**, **ool**, and **oke**)

Make: owl low pow plow slow loop pool wool woke poke
spoke spool spook slowpoke

Sort:

low	pow	pool	woke
slow	plow	spool	poke
		wool	spoke
			slowpoke

Transfer: drool   joke   grow   slow

Make Words

- Have children name and hold up letters.
- Tell children how many letters to use to make each word.
- Have children say each word and stretch out some words.
- Give sentences to clarify meaning.
- Give specific instructions on how to change words:
  — Add one letter.
  — Change the first letter.
  — Use the same letters.
- Have children clear their holders before making an unrelated word.
- Have children correct their word once it is made in the pocket chart.
- Give children one minute to figure out the secret word and then give them clues.

Sort Words

- Put words in pocket chart in the order made.
- Have children say and spell each word.
- Remind them of how each word was changed to spell the new word.
- Select one word from each rhyming set and line up in columns.
- Let children choose the other words that rhyme.
- Have children pronounce the words.

Transfer Words

- Tell children that they are going to use the rhyming words to spell some new words they might need when they are writing.
- Say the word and a sentence one of your children might write.
- Have children say the word and decide on the beginning letters.
- Write the beginning letters on an index card.
- Take the index card with the beginning letters to the pocket chart and have children say the columns of rhymes and the new word to find the rhyming pattern.
- Write the rhyming pattern on the card to finish the word.
- Have students write the word on paper or a whiteboard.

Lesson 87

snowballs

Letters: a o b l l n s s w (Patterns **aw**, **ow**, and **all**)

Make: all saw law low snow slow blow lawn ball fall hall allow snowballs

Sort:

saw	low	all
law	snow	fall
	blow	hall
	slow	ball

Transfer: claw straw glow small tow

Make Words

- Have children name and hold up letters.
- Tell children how many letters to use to make each word.
- Have children say each word and stretch out some words.
- Give sentences to clarify meaning.
- Give specific instructions on how to change words:
  — Add one letter.
  — Change the first letter.
  — Use the same letters.
- Have children clear their holders before making an unrelated word.
- Have children correct their word once it is made in the pocket chart.
- Give children one minute to figure out the secret word and then give them clues.

Sort Words

- Put words in pocket chart in the order made.
- Have children say and spell each word.
- Remind them of how each word was changed to spell the new word.
- Select one word from each rhyming set and line up in columns.
- Let children choose the other words that rhyme.
- Have children pronounce the words.

Transfer Words

- Tell children that they are going to use the rhyming words to spell some new words they might need when they are writing.
- Say the word and a sentence one of your children might write.
- Have children say the word and decide on the beginning letters.
- Write the beginning letters on an index card.
- Take the index card with the beginning letters to the pocket chart and have children say the columns of rhymes and the new word to find the rhyming pattern.
- Write the rhyming pattern on the card to finish the word.
- Have students write the word on paper or a whiteboard.

Lesson 88

snowflake

Letters: | a | e | o | f | k | l | n | s | w | (Patterns **aw** and **ow**)

Make: saw law low slow slaw lawn snow flow leak weak
wake lake flake snake snowflake

Sort:

saw	slow	leak	lake
slaw	snow	weak	wake
law	flow		flake
			snake
			snowflake

Transfer: draw   throw   straw   rake

Make Words

- Have children name and hold up letters.
- Tell children how many letters to use to make each word.
- Have children say each word and stretch out some words.
- Give sentences to clarify meaning.
- Give specific instructions on how to change words:
  — Add one letter.
  — Change the first letter.
  — Use the same letters.
- Have children clear their holders before making an unrelated word.
- Have children correct their word once it is made in the pocket chart.
- Give children one minute to figure out the secret word and then give them clues.

Sort Words

- Put words in pocket chart in the order made.
- Have children say and spell each word.
- Remind them of how each word was changed to spell the new word.
- Select one word from each rhyming set and line up in columns.
- Let children choose the other words that rhyme.
- Have children pronounce the words.

Transfer Words

- Tell children that they are going to use the rhyming words to spell some new words they might need when they are writing.
- Say the word and a sentence one of your children might write.
- Have children say the word and decide on the beginning letters.
- Write the beginning letters on an index card.
- Take the index card with the beginning letters to the pocket chart and have children say the columns of rhymes and the new word to find the rhyming pattern.
- Write the rhyming pattern on the card to finish the word.
- Have students write the word on paper or a whiteboard.

strawberry

Letters: a e b r r r s t w y (Patterns **aw**, **eat**, **est**, and **east**)

Make: saw raw wet set bet beat seat east rest west
best beast straw arrest strawberry

Sort:

saw	beat	set	best	east
raw	seat	wet	west	beast
straw		bet	rest	

Transfer: feast draw least test claw

Make Words

- Have children name and hold up letters.
- Tell children how many letters to use to make each word.
- Have children say each word and stretch out some words.
- Give sentences to clarify meaning.
- Give specific instructions on how to change words:
  — Add one letter.
  — Change the first letter.
  — Use the same letters.
- Have children clear their holders before making an unrelated word.
- Have children correct their word once it is made in the pocket chart.
- Give children one minute to figure out the secret word and then give them clues.

Sort Words

- Put words in pocket chart in the order made.
- Have children say and spell each word.
- Remind them of how each word was changed to spell the new word.
- Select one word from each rhyming set and line up in columns.
- Let children choose the other words that rhyme.
- Have children pronounce the words.

Transfer Words

- Tell children that they are going to use the rhyming words to spell some new words they might need when they are writing.
- Say the word and a sentence one of your children might write.
- Have children say the word and decide on the beginning letters.
- Write the beginning letters on an index card.
- Take the index card with the beginning letters to the pocket chart and have children say the columns of rhymes and the new word to find the rhyming pattern.
- Write the rhyming pattern on the card to finish the word.
- Have students write the word on paper or a whiteboard.

Lesson 90

thankful

Letters: | a | u | f | h | k | l | n | t | (Patterns **at**, **ut**, and **ank**)

Make: hat   sat   Nat   nut   hut   hunt   flat   tank   Hank   haul
haunt   fault   thank   thankful

Sort:

nut	tank	hat
hut	Hank	sat
	thank	Nat
		flat

Transfer: plank   blank   scat   shut

Make Words

- Have children name and hold up letters.
- Tell children how many letters to use to make each word.
- Have children say each word and stretch out some words.
- Give sentences to clarify meaning.
- Give specific instructions on how to change words:
  — Add one letter.
  — Change the first letter.
  — Use the same letters.
- Have children clear their holders before making an unrelated word.
- Have children correct their word once it is made in the pocket chart.
- Give children one minute to figure out the secret word and then give them clues.

Sort Words

- Put words in pocket chart in the order made.
- Have children say and spell each word.
- Remind them of how each word was changed to spell the new word.
- Select one word from each rhyming set and line up in columns.
- Let children choose the other words that rhyme.
- Have children pronounce the words.

Transfer Words

- Tell children that they are going to use the rhyming words to spell some new words they might need when they are writing.
- Say the word and a sentence one of your children might write.
- Have children say the word and decide on the beginning letters.
- Write the beginning letters on an index card.
- Take the index card with the beginning letters to the pocket chart and have children say the columns of rhymes and the new word to find the rhyming pattern.
- Write the rhyming pattern on the card to finish the word.
- Have students write the word on paper or a whiteboard.

Tell the children to pretend they are writing and need to spell some words. To spell the word, they should stretch out the word and write the beginning letters and then decide which rhyming words will help them finish writing the word. Write these words in columns and have your students chorally pronounce and spell them.

all	bell	hill
tall	sell	pill
ball	tell	bill

Have the children number a sheet of paper from 1 to 5. Say a word and put it in a sentence. Ask your students to stretch out each word to hear the beginning letters and then decide which words it rhymes with to finish spelling the word:

thrill   stall   smell   drill   swell

Record their responses on your record sheet. If students did not use the correct pattern or beginning letters, record what they did use and analyze their errors.

Word	Beginning Letters	Rhyming Pattern
After Lesson 10		
drip	dr	ip
yet	y	et
chop	ch	op
skip	sk	ip
crop	cr	op
After Lesson 20		
thick	th	ick
check	ch	eck
shock	sh	ock
brick	br	ick
clock	cl	ock
After Lesson 30		
flight	fl	ight
shine	sh	ine
bride	br	ide
spine	sp	ine
slight	sl	ight

Word	Beginning Letters	Rhyming Pattern
After Lesson 40		
plate	pl	ate
stray	str	ay
grain	gr	ain
spray	spr	ay
chain	ch	ain
After Lesson 50		
bleed	bl	eed
shame	sh	ame
scream	scr	eam
greed	gr	eed
stream	str	eam
After Lesson 60		
true	tr	ue
spun	sp	un
prune	pr	une
glue	gl	ue
stun	st	un
After Lesson 70		
smart	sm	art
short	sh	ort
score	sc	ore
chore	ch	ore
snore	sn	ore
After Lesson 80		
spool	sp	ool
snail	sn	ail
stool	st	ool
broil	br	oil
drool	dr	ool

Word	Beginning Letters	Rhyming Pattern
After Lesson 90		
thrill	thr	ill
stall	st	all
smell	sm	ell
drill	sr	ill
swell	sw	ell

Lessons 91-100

These 10 lessons review the common vowel patterns taught in the lessons in this book.

Lesson 91

meatballs

Letters: a a e b l l m s t   (Patterns **eat**, **eam**, **ame**, **ate**, and **east**)

Words to Make: eat   meat/mate/tame/team   beam   beat   late   lame
blame   beast   least   steal   tamales   meatballs

Part One • Making Words

Have the children arrange their letters in front of their holders to match the pocket-chart letters, with the vowel first and the other letters in alphabetical order. Ask the children to hold up and name each letter, noting the capital letter is used to spell names.

eat "The first word we are going to spell is **eat**. What did you **eat** for breakfast? Everyone say **eat**. Use 3 letters to spell **eat**."

Choose a child who has **eat** spelled correctly to spell **eat** with the pocket-chart letters. Have the class chorally spell **eat** and fix their word if **eat** is not correct.

meat "Add 1 letter to spell **meat**. What kind of **meat** do you like? Everyone say **meat**."

Let a child who has **meat** spelled correctly spell **meat** with the pocket-chart letters.

mate "Move the letters to spell **mate**. Some animals **mate** for life. Everyone say **mate**."

Continue the lesson, giving children explicit instruction about which letters to remove and where to add letters. Put each word in a sentence and have children say each word before making it. Have them "stretch" some words to provide practice for children who are still learning to segment words. Let a child who has spelled the word correctly

make that word with the pocket-chart letters. Choose your struggling readers when the word is an easy word and your advanced readers for harder words. Have the children chorally spell each word after it is made in the pocket chart and fix their word to match.

tame	"Move the letters to spell **tame**. The man has a **tame** monkey for a pet. Everyone say **tame**."
team	"Use the same letters to spell **team**. My brother is on my **team**. Everyone say **team**."
beam	"Change the first letter to spell **beam**. Can you walk on the balance **beam**? Everyone say **beam**."
beat	"Change 1 letter to spell **beat**. My favorite team **beat** my husband's favorite team. Everyone say **beat**."
late	"Use 4 letters to spell **late**. Please don't be **late**. Everyone say **late**."
lame	"Change 1 letter to spell **lame**. The pony hurt her leg and was **lame**. Everyone say **lame**."
blame	"Add 1 letter to spell **blame**. Don't **blame** me for the bad weather. Everyone say **blame**."
beast	"Use 5 letters to spell **beast**. The campers were frightened by a wild **beast**. Everyone say **beast**."
least	"Change 1 letter to spell **least**. I was late to the party but at **least** I got there in time for dessert. Everyone say **least**."
steal	"Move the letters to spell **steal**. It is wrong to **steal** things. Everyone say **steal**."
tamales	"Use 7 letters to spell **tamales**. Have you ever eaten **tamales**? Everyone say **tamales**."
meatballs	**(the secret word)** "It's time for the secret word. Signal me if you can figure it out and make it in your holder."

If no one figures out the secret word in one minute, give them a clue.

End the making words part of the lesson by having someone spell **meatballs** in the pocket chart and letting everyone hold up their holders to show you **meatballs** made in their holders. Have them close the holders and turn their attention to the pocket chart.

Part Two • Sorting Words (Sort for **eat**, **ate**, **ame**, **eam**, and **east**)

Using the index cards with the words, place them in the pocket chart and have the children pronounce them. Remind them of what they changed to make each word.

"First we used 3 letters to spell **eat**, e-a-t."

"We added 1 letter to spell **meat**, m-e-a-t."

"We used the same letters to spell **mate**, m-a-t-e."

"We used the same letters again to spell **tame**, t-a-m-e."

"We moved the letters to spell **team**, t-e-a-m."

"We changed 1 letter to spell **beam**, b-e-a-m."

"We changed the last letter to spell **beat**, **b-e-a-t**."

"We used 4 letters to spell **late**, **l-a-t-e**."

"We changed 1 letter to spell **lame**, **l-a-m-e**."

"We used 5 letters to spell **blame**, **b-l-a-m-e**."

"We used 5 letters to spell **beast**, **b-e-a-s-t**."

"We changed a letter to spell **least**, **l-e-a-s-t**."

"We used the same letters to spell **steal**, **s-t-e-a-l**."

"We used 7 letters to spell **tamales**, **t-a-m-a-l-e-s**."

"We used all our letters to spell the secret word, **meatballs**, **m-e-a-t-b-a-l-l-s**."

"Now we need to sort out the rhymes. I will take one of each set and you can come and help me find the others."

Arrange one of each set of rhyming words to begin five columns.

eat	mate	tame	team	least

Choose five children to find the other rhyming words.

eat	mate	tame	team	least
meat	late	lame	beam	beast
beat	blame			

Part Three • Transfer dream cream scream same cheat

Have the children take out paper. Tell them that you are going to say a word that someone might be writing. By figuring out the rhyming pattern, they will be able to spell the word.

"The first word we are going to spell is **dream**. Jen might be writing about what happened in her **dream**. Let's all say **dream** and listen for the beginning letters."

Write **dr** on an index card. Take the index card to the pocket chart and have the children pronounce **dream** with each set of rhyming words. When they decide that **dream** rhymes with **team** and **beam**, write **eam** next to **dr**. Have children write **dream** on their papers.

Repeat this procedure for **cream**, **scream**, **same**, and **cheat**.

Lesson 92

brightest

Letters: `e` `i` `b` `g` `h` `r` `s` `t` `t`   (Patterns **it**, **ir**, **ire**, and **ight**)

Make: fit sit sir stir hire tire tight sight right tribe birth
thirst bright brightest

Sort:

fit	sir	tire	tight
sit	stir	hire	sight
			right
			bright

Transfer: slight wire fright flight skit

Make Words

- Have children name and hold up letters.
- Tell children how many letters to use to make each word.
- Have children say each word and stretch out some words.
- Give sentences to clarify meaning.
- Give specific instructions on how to change words:
  — Add one letter.
  — Change the first letter.
  — Use the same letters.
- Have children clear their holders before making an unrelated word.
- Have children correct their word once it is made in the pocket chart.
- Give children one minute to figure out the secret word and then give them clues.

Sort Words

- Put words in pocket chart in the order made.
- Have children say and spell each word.
- Remind them of how each word was changed to spell the new word.
- Select one word from each rhyming set and line up in columns.
- Let children choose the other words that rhyme.
- Have children pronounce the words.

Transfer Words

- Tell children that they are going to use the rhyming words to spell some new words they might need when they are writing.
- Say the word and a sentence one of your children might write.
- Have children say the word and decide on the beginning letters.
- Write the beginning letters on an index card.
- Take the index card with the beginning letters to the pocket chart and have children say the columns of rhymes and the new word to find the rhyming pattern.
- Write the rhyming pattern on the card to finish the word.
- Have students write the word on paper or a whiteboard.

Lesson 93

friendly

Letters: e i d f l n r y (Patterns **y** and **ine**)

Make: dry fry fly rely deny defy dine fine line life
file rifle friend friendly

Sort:

dry	dine
fly	fine
fly	
rely	
deny	

Transfer: shine   spy   spine   twine   nine

Make Words

- Have children name and hold up letters.
- Tell children how many letters to use to make each word.
- Have children say each word and stretch out some words.
- Give sentences to clarify meaning.
- Give specific instructions on how to change words:
  — Add one letter.
  — Change the first letter.
  — Use the same letters.
- Have children clear their holders before making an unrelated word.
- Have children correct their word once it is made in the pocket chart.
- Give children one minute to figure out the secret word and then give them clues.

Sort Words

- Put words in pocket chart in the order made.
- Have children say and spell each word.
- Remind them of how each word was changed to spell the new word.
- Select one word from each rhyming set and line up in columns.
- Let children choose the other words that rhyme.
- Have children pronounce the words.

Transfer Words

- Tell children that they are going to use the rhyming words to spell some new words they might need when they are writing.
- Say the word and a sentence one of your children might write.
- Have children say the word and decide on the beginning letters.
- Write the beginning letters on an index card.
- Take the index card with the beginning letters to the pocket chart and have children say the columns of rhymes and the new word to find the rhyming pattern.
- Write the rhyming pattern on the card to finish the word.
- Have students write the word on paper or a whiteboard.

Lesson 94

helicopter

Letters: | e | e | i | o | c | h | l | p | r | t | (Patterns **ore**, **ole**, **ope**, and **orch**)

Make: her hero port core tore pole role hole hope rope elope torch porch polite helicopter

Sort:

core	role	rope	porch
tore	pole	hope	torch
	hole	elope	

Transfer: score scope scorch slope

Make Words

- Have children name and hold up letters.
- Tell children how many letters to use to make each word.
- Have children say each word and stretch out some words.
- Give sentences to clarify meaning.
- Give specific instructions on how to change words:
  — Add one letter.
  — Change the first letter.
  — Use the same letters.
- Have children clear their holders before making an unrelated word.
- Have children correct their word once it is made in the pocket chart.
- Give children one minute to figure out the secret word and then give them clues.

Sort Words

- Put words in pocket chart in the order made.
- Have children say and spell each word.
- Remind them of how each word was changed to spell the new word.
- Select one word from each rhyming set and line up in columns.
- Let children choose the other words that rhyme.
- Have children pronounce the words.

Transfer Words

- Tell children that they are going to use the rhyming words to spell some new words they might need when they are writing.
- Say the word and a sentence one of your children might write.
- Have children say the word and decide on the beginning letters.
- Write the beginning letters on an index card.
- Take the index card with the beginning letters to the pocket chart and have children say the columns of rhymes and the new word to find the rhyming pattern.
- Write the rhyming pattern on the card to finish the word.
- Have students write the word on paper or a whiteboard.

Lesson 95

computers

Letters: | e | o | u | c | m | p | r | s | t | (Patterns **our**, **out**, **ost**, and **ute**)

Make: our   out   pout   poet   poem   post   most   cute   mute   sour
scour   scout   costume   customer   computers

Sort:

our	out	post	mute
sour	scout	most	cute
scour	pout		

Transfer: spout   host   flour   sprout   flute

Make Words

- Have children name and hold up letters.
- Tell children how many letters to use to make each word.
- Have children say each word and stretch out some words.
- Give sentences to clarify meaning.
- Give specific instructions on how to change words:
  — Add one letter.
  — Change the first letter.
  — Use the same letters.
- Have children clear their holders before making an unrelated word.
- Have children correct their word once it is made in the pocket chart.
- Give children one minute to figure out the secret word and then give them clues.

Sort Words

- Put words in pocket chart in the order made.
- Have children say and spell each word.
- Remind them of how each word was changed to spell the new word.
- Select one word from each rhyming set and line up in columns.
- Let children choose the other words that rhyme.
- Have children pronounce the words.

Transfer Words

- Tell children that they are going to use the rhyming words to spell some new words they might need when they are writing.
- Say the word and a sentence one of your children might write.
- Have children say the word and decide on the beginning letters.
- Write the beginning letters on an index card.
- Take the index card with the beginning letters to the pocket chart and have children say the columns of rhymes and the new word to find the rhyming pattern.
- Write the rhyming pattern on the card to finish the word.
- Have students write the word on paper or a whiteboard.

136

Lesson 96

raindrops

Letters: | a | i | o | d | n | r | r | p | s | (Patterns **ad**, **aid**, **on**, **an**, and **ain**)

Make: ad aid ran Ron Don Dan pan pad paid pain rain
drain Spain sprain raindrops

Sort:

aid	ad	Ron	Dan	pain
paid	pad	Don	ran	rain
				drain
				Spain
				sprain

Transfer: brain   braid   Brad   bran

Make Words

- Have children name and hold up letters.
- Tell children how many letters to use to make each word.
- Have children say each word and stretch out some words.
- Give sentences to clarify meaning.
- Give specific instructions on how to change words:
  — Add one letter.
  — Change the first letter.
  — Use the same letters.
- Have children clear their holders before making an unrelated word.
- Make sure children use capital letters when spelling names.
- Have children correct their word once it is made in the pocket chart.
- Give children one minute to figure out the secret word and then give them clues.

Sort Words

- Put words in pocket chart in the order made.
- Have children say and spell each word.
- Remind them of how each word was changed to spell the new word.
- Select one word from each rhyming set and line up in columns.
- Let children choose the other words that rhyme.
- Have children pronounce the words.

Transfer Words

- Tell children that they are going to use the rhyming words to spell some new words they might need when they are writing.
- Say the word and a sentence one of your children might write.
- Have children say the word and decide on the beginning letters.
- Write the beginning letters on an index card.
- Take the index card with the beginning letters to the pocket chart and have children say the columns of rhymes and the new word to find the rhyming pattern.
- Write the rhyming pattern on the card to finish the word.
- Have students write the word on paper or a whiteboard.

dumpster

Letters: | e | u | d | m | p | r | s | t | (Patterns **ump**, **ust**, and **ure**)

Make:
drum   dump   dust   rust   pure   sure   mute   spurt   stump
rusted   rudest   purest   stumped   spurted   dumpster

Sort:
| dump | dust | pure |
| stump | rust | sure |

Transfer: cure   crust   slump   clump

Make Words

- Have children name and hold up letters.
- Tell children how many letters to use to make each word.
- Have children say each word and stretch out some words.
- Give sentences to clarify meaning.
- Give specific instructions on how to change words:
  — Add one letter.
  — Change the first letter.
  — Use the same letters.
- Have children clear their holders before making an unrelated word.
- Have children correct their word once it is made in the pocket chart.
- Give children one minute to figure out the secret word and then give them clues.

Sort Words

- Put words in pocket chart in the order made.
- Have children say and spell each word.
- Remind them of how each word was changed to spell the new word.
- Select one word from each rhyming set and line up in columns.
- Let children choose the other words that rhyme.
- Have children pronounce the words.

Transfer Words

- Tell children that they are going to use the rhyming words to spell some new words they might need when they are writing.
- Say the word and a sentence one of your children might write.
- Have children say the word and decide on the beginning letters.
- Write the beginning letters on an index card.
- Take the index card with the beginning letters to the pocket chart and have children say the columns of rhymes and the new word to find the rhyming pattern.
- Write the rhyming pattern on the card to finish the word.
- Have students write the word on paper or a whiteboard.

Lesson 98

rectangle

Letters: | a | e | e | c | g | l | n | r | t | (Patterns **age**, **ace**, and **angle**)

Make: can age ace lace race rage cage cent angle tangle
center recent cereal central rectangle

Sort:

age	race	angle
rage	ace	tangle
cage	lace	

Transfer: dangle   space   page   stage   place

Make Words

- Have children name and hold up letters.
- Tell children how many letters to use to make each word.
- Have children say each word and stretch out some words.
- Give sentences to clarify meaning.
- Give specific instructions on how to change words:
  — Add one letter.
  — Change the first letter.
  — Use the same letters.
- Have children clear their holders before making an unrelated word.
- Have children correct their word once it is made in the pocket chart.
- Give children one minute to figure out the secret word and then give them clues.

Sort Words

- Put words in pocket chart in the order made.
- Have children say and spell each word.
- Remind them of how each word was changed to spell the new word.
- Select one word from each rhyming set and line up in columns.
- Let children choose the other words that rhyme.
- Have children pronounce the words.

Transfer Words

- Tell children that they are going to use the rhyming words to spell some new words they might need when they are writing.
- Say the word and a sentence one of your children might write.
- Have children say the word and decide on the beginning letters.
- Write the beginning letters on an index card.
- Take the index card with the beginning letters to the pocket chart and have children say the columns of rhymes and the new word to find the rhyming pattern.
- Write the rhyming pattern on the card to finish the word.
- Have students write the word on paper or a whiteboard.

Lesson 99

managers

Letters: a a e g m n r s (Patterns **an**, **ag**, **age**, and **ame**)

Make: men man ran rag nag sag age rage game same name
mean manage manager managers

Sort:

man	rag	age	name
ran	nag	rage	game
	sag		same

Transfer: shame stage frame wage flag

Make Words

- Have children name and hold up letters.
- Tell children how many letters to use to make each word.
- Have children say each word and stretch out some words.
- Give sentences to clarify meaning.
- Give specific instructions on how to change words:
  — Add one letter.
  — Change the first letter.
  — Use the same letters.
- Have children clear their holders before making an unrelated word.
- Have children correct their word once it is made in the pocket chart.
- Give children one minute to figure out the secret word and then give them clues.

Sort Words

- Put words in pocket chart in the order made.
- Have children say and spell each word.
- Remind them of how each word was changed to spell the new word.
- Select one word from each rhyming set and line up in columns.
- Let children choose the other words that rhyme.
- Have children pronounce the words.

Transfer Words

- Tell children that they are going to use the rhyming words to spell some new words they might need when they are writing.
- Say the word and a sentence one of your children might write.
- Have children say the word and decide on the beginning letters.
- Write the beginning letters on an index card.
- Take the index card with the beginning letters to the pocket chart and have children say the columns of rhymes and the new word to find the rhyming pattern.
- Write the rhyming pattern on the card to finish the word.
- Have students write the word on paper or a whiteboard.

racetrack

Letters: | a | a | e | c | c | k | r | r | t | (Patterns **at**, **ate**, **ack**, and **ace**)

Make: at ate ace rat car care race rack rate crate
track crack cracker racecar racetrack

Sort:

rat	ate	rack	race
at	rate	track	ace
	crate	crack	

Transfer: brace   shack   trace   Grace   flat

Make Words

- Have children name and hold up letters.
- Tell children how many letters to use to make each word.
- Have children say each word and stretch out some words.
- Give sentences to clarify meaning.
- Give specific instructions on how to change words:
  — Add one letter.
  — Change the first letter.
  — Use the same letters.
- Have children clear their holders before making an unrelated word.
- Have children correct their word once it is made in the pocket chart.
- Give children one minute to figure out the secret word and then give them clues.

Sort Words

- Put words in pocket chart in the order made.
- Have children say and spell each word.
- Remind them of how each word was changed to spell the new word.
- Select one word from each rhyming set and line up in columns.
- Let children choose the other words that rhyme.
- Have children pronounce the words.

Transfer Words

- Tell children that they are going to use the rhyming words to spell some new words they might need when they are writing.
- Say the word and a sentence one of your children might write.
- Have children say the word and decide on the beginning letters.
- Write the beginning letters on an index card.
- Take the index card with the beginning letters to the pocket chart and have children say the columns of rhymes and the new word to find the rhyming pattern.
- Write the rhyming pattern on the card to finish the word.
- Have students write the word on paper or a whiteboard.

Assessment Lessons 91-100

Tell the children to pretend they are writing and need to spell some words. To spell the word, they should stretch out the word and write the beginning letters and then decide which rhyming words will help them finish writing the word. Write these words in columns and have your students pronounce and spell them.

meat	night	ate
eat	right	gate
beat	sight	late

Have the children number a sheet of paper from 1 to 5. Say a word and put it in a sentence. Ask your students to stretch out each word to hear the beginning letters and then decide which words it rhymes with to finish spelling the word:

flight   cheat   skate   bright   plate

Record their responses on your record sheet. If students did not use the correct pattern or beginning letters, record what they did use and analyze their errors.

Word	Beginning Letters	Rhyming Pattern
After Lesson 10		
drip	dr	ip
yet	y	et
chop	ch	op
skip	sk	ip
crop	cr	op
After Lesson 20		
thick	th	ick
check	ch	eck
shock	sh	ock
brick	br	ick
clock	cl	ock
After Lesson 30		
flight	fl	ight
shine	sh	ine
bride	br	ide
spine	sp	ine
slight	sl	ight

Word	Beginning Letters	Rhyming Pattern
After Lesson 40		
plate	pl	ate
stray	str	ay
grain	gr	ain
spray	spr	ay
chain	ch	ain
After Lesson 50		
bleed	bl	eed
shame	sh	ame
scream	scr	eam
greed	gr	eed
stream	str	eam
After Lesson 60		
true	tr	ue
spun	sp	un
prune	pr	une
glue	gl	ue
stun	st	un
After Lesson 70		
smart	sm	art
short	sh	ort
score	sc	ore
chore	ch	ore
snore	sn	ore
After Lesson 80		
spool	sp	ool
snail	sn	ail
stool	st	ool
broil	br	oil
drool	dr	ool

Word	Beginning Letters	Rhyming Pattern
After Lesson 90		
thrill	thr	ill
stall	st	all
smell	sm	ell
drill	sr	ill
swell	sw	ell
After Lesson 100		
flight	fl	ight
cheat	ch	eat
skate	sk	ate
bright	br	ight
plate	pl	ate

Reproducible Letters

Reproducible Consonants

Copy on white card stock, making twice as many letters as you have children.

Reproducible Vowels

Copy on a different color card stock, making twice as many letters as you have children.

Reproducible Y

Y is sometimes a consonant and sometimes a vowel. Copy on a different color card stock, making twice as many letters as you have children.

b	c	d	f	g	h
b	c	d	f	g	h
b	c	d	f	g	h
b	c	d	f	g	h

H	G	F	D	C	B
H	G	F	D	C	B
H	G	F	D	C	B
H	G	F	D	C	B

j	k	l	m	n	p
j	k	l	m	n	p
j	k	l	m	n	p
j	k	l	m	n	p

P	N	M	L	K	J
P	N	M	L	K	J
P	N	M	L	K	J
P	N	M	L	K	J

q	r	s	t	v	w
q	r	s	t	v	w
q	r	s	t	v	w
q	r	s	t	v	w

W	V	T	S	R	Q
W	V	T	S	R	Q
W	V	T	S	R	Q
W	V	T	S	R	Q

x	z	n	r	s	t
x	z	n	r	s	t
x	z	n	r	s	t
x	z	n	r	s	t

T	S	R	N	Z	X
T	S	R	N	Z	X
T	S	R	N	Z	X
T	S	R	N	Z	X

a	e	i	o	u	a
a	e	i	o	u	e
a	e	i	o	u	i
a	e	i	o	u	o

A	U	O	I	E	A
E	U	O	I	E	A
I	U	O	I	E	A
O	U	O	I	E	A

y	y	y	y	y	y
y	y	y	y	y	y
y	y	y	y	y	y
y	y	y	y	y	y

Y	Y	Y	Y	Y	Y
Y	Y	Y	Y	Y	Y
Y	Y	Y	Y	Y	Y
Y	Y	Y	Y	Y	Y

Reproducible Record Sheet

Word	Beginning Letters	Rhyming Pattern
After Lesson 10		
drip	dr	ip
yet	y	et
chop	ch	op
skip	sk	ip
crop	cr	op
After Lesson 20		
thick	th	ick
check	ch	eck
shock	sh	ock
brick	br	ick
clock	cl	ock
After Lesson 30		
flight	fl	ight
shine	sh	ine
bride	br	ide
spine	sp	ine
slight	sl	ight
After Lesson 40		
plate	pl	ate
stray	str	ay
grain	gr	ain
spray	spr	ay
chain	ch	ain
After Lesson 50		
bleed	bl	eed
shame	sh	ame
scream	scr	eam
greed	gr	eed
stream	str	eam

Word	Beginning Letters	Rhyming Pattern
After Lesson 60		
true	tr	ue
spun	sp	un
prune	pr	une
glue	gl	ue
stun	st	un
After Lesson 70		
smart	sm	art
short	sh	ort
score	sc	ore
chore	ch	ore
snore	sn	ore
After Lesson 80		
spool	sp	ool
snail	sn	ail
stool	st	ool
broil	br	oil
drool	dr	ool
After Lesson 90		
thrill	thr	ill
stall	st	all
smell	sm	ell
drill	sr	ill
swell	sw	ell
After Lesson 100		
flight	fl	ight
cheat	ch	eat
skate	sk	ate
bright	br	ight
plate	pl	ate

Reproducible Making Words Take-Home Sheet